BY HIMSELF
The Older Man's Experience
of Widowhood

DEBORAH K. VAN DEN HOONAARD

By Himself

The Older Man's Experience of Widowhood

UNIVERSITY OF TORONTO PRESS
Toronto Buffalo London

© University of Toronto Press Incorporated 2010
Toronto Buffalo London
www.utppublishing.com
Printed in Canada

ISBN 978-1-4426-4109-9

Library and Archives Canada Cataloguing in Publication

Van den Hoonaard, Deborah K. (Deborah Kestin), 1951–
By himself: the older man's experience of widowhood / Deborah K. van den Hoonaard.

Includes bibliographical references and index.
ISBN 978-1-4426-4109-9

1. Widowers – Canada – Social conditions. 2. Widowers – United States – Social conditions. 3. Widowers – Canada – Biography. 4. Widowers – United States – Biography. 5. Widowers – Canada – Interviews. 6. Widowers – United States – Interviews. I. Title.

HQ1058.5.C3V35 2010   306.88'20971   C2009-907071-5

This book is published with the assistance of a grant from the Atlantic Centre for Qualitative Research and Analysis of St Thomas University.

University of Toronto Press acknowledges the financial assistance to its publishing program of the Canada Council for the Arts and the Ontario Arts Council.

 Canada Council **Conseil des Arts**
for the Arts **du Canada**

 ONTARIO ARTS COUNCIL
CONSEIL DES ARTS DE L'ONTARIO

University of Toronto Press acknowledges the financial support for its publishing activities of the Government of Canada through the Book Publishing Industry Development Program (BPIDP).

To my three children, Lisa-Jo, Cheryl, and Jordan –
who have taken me places I never thought I would go
with love

One of the strangers who arrived at the station a few years ago was Jarvis Poulter ... [His] house is plainer than the Roth house and has no fruit trees or flowers planted around it. It is understood that this is a natural result of Jarvis Poulter's being a widower and living alone. A man may keep his house decent, but he will never – if he is a proper man – do much to decorate it. Marriage forces him to live with more ornament as well as sentiment, and it protects him, also, from the extremities of his own nature – from a frigid parsimony or a luxuriant sloth, from squalor, and from excessive sleeping, drinking, smoking or free thinking.

Alice Munro, 'Menesteung' (2000[1989]).

THE WIDOWER

Already he saw it all,
rocked back against his tobacco counter, staring out
in the barred window of his grocery
at the highway and the green wilderness of kudzu
quilting the hills beyond.
Often a customer standing inside the door
had to shuffle or cough, or a stranger in a hurry
might slap the top of the Coke box.
I raided the ice-cream cooler a hundred times.

On hot days, a fan turned its slow head
in a corner, and in winter
the fat stove sighed over the oiled floor.
A gospel quartet always sang on the radio,
promises that may have signified.
For a clean and high tenor
his head might tilt,
and he rarely moved unless he had to.

The spirit had simply retired to a chair
for a reverie of twenty years,
as though he'd found a window into himself,
or out. And only occasionally,
when the store was empty, would he turn
to check the register or the meat freezer,
the aisle behind the dress patterns
and the racks of thread,
the way a traveler broken down in the country
will look up the road
for help he knows is not coming,
or a man, who's lost a good watch
will continue to glance
at his wrist.

David Bottoms (1996)

Contents

x   Contents

Acknowledgments

The research and writing of this book was like finding myself in a foreign land. Many people helped me to navigate the new territory and supported my efforts. An author may write a book alone, but she stands on the shoulders of colleagues, friends, teachers, and family.

First, thanks go to the men who shared their stories with me. They guided me through the new terrain and were generous with their accounts and with their time. They shared many confidences. This book could not exist without the chance the participants took when they volunteered to be interviewed.

Widowers are very difficult to find, and I could not have completed the research without the help of friends and family who referred me to widowers whom they knew. I cannot identify this group by name without compromising the confidentiality of the widowers, but I am very grateful to them.

Also helpful were the local media who publicized my research. CBC's *Maritime Noon* telephoned me to request an interview as soon as the grant for the study was made public. When I emailed *Main Street* to request that they interview me, I was on the air that afternoon! The *Daily Gleaner* and Rogers Cable also brought attention to the study.

Many colleagues encouraged me with their continuing interest, sticking with it for a long time. The members of the Department of Gerontology at St Thomas University, Linda Caissie, Gary Irwin-Kenyon, and Bill Randall, all celebrate each other's accomplishments, and for this I am grateful. Other colleagues at St Thomas University, the late John McKendy, Michelle Lafrance, and Dawne Clarke have followed the development of the book with great interest. Marianne Skarborn has been a constant support and has always attended talks and papers that I gave and generously shared her insights. Janet Stoppard, friend and research partner, has been a staunch supporter of my work.

John McKendy, in particular, took the time to read drafts of early papers and discuss my emerging ideas about men's widowhood and masculinity. He personified encouraging collegiality and was one of the few people who challenged my ideas critically. My work is much better as a result of our discussions. His untimely passing is a great loss to all of us.

Rosemary Clews, past Assistant Vice-President (Research) at St Thomas University, never failed to share her enthusiasm for all of our successes, and this one is no different. Her contributions to establishing an atmosphere that encourages research at St Thomas University have facilitated all the research aspirations of the faculty. She has celebrated every accomplishment of the research with me, from the announcement of my getting a grant to the finishing of this book.

Thanks also go to administrative assistants extraordinaire Penny Granter, John Stringer, and Donna Beek. Students Catherine Swail and Shannon Brown read novels about widowers for me, and Sarah Laidley helped with the background reading. Students in my classes have been very interested in my research, and their questions and suggested interpretations always stimulated my thinking.

When the issue of masculinity eventually emerged as an important component of this study, a number of people helped me to develop my thinking in the area. James Messerschmidt of the University of Southern Maine met me for lunch to talk about masculinity. Ian Nicholson of the Psychology Department at St Thomas University responded positively to my request to give a talk in his seminar on masculinity. In Israel, Gabriela Spector-Mercel's work on older men and masculinity scripts was very helpful and has led to our commencing a warm friendship via email. At Carleton University, Andrea Doucet's book *Do Men Mother?* came out just in time for me to include some of her insights about the situation of a woman interviewing men. Her metaphor of gossamer walls turned on a light in my own interpretation of my relationship with my interview participants.

The small community of those who study the social meaning of widowhood for older men has been a true gift. Kate Davidson, Dorothy Stratton, Alinde Moore, and Kate Bennett, in particular, have been eager to share ideas about my and their research.

Much of the data first saw the light of day at the annual Canadian Qualitatives conference. I am grateful to the community of qualitative researchers who meet annually to provide support and encouragement to one another. I never fail to return from the conference with renewed energy and ideas. Dan and Cheryl Albas, in particular, have become valued friends and have generously offered thoughts and concepts that have enriched my analysis.

Although I finished my PhD fifteen years ago, I still owe a debt of gratitude to those who mentored me through that process. Their intellectual contributions to my work continue. My supervisor, Helena Z. Lopata, the first to study widowhood in North America, both inspired and prodded me on to a higher standard. Christine L. Fry and Judith Wittner at Loyola University of Chicago have each added in her own way to my growth as a scholar. Howard S. Becker welcomed me into his field-methods class at Northwestern University, and I am regularly struck by the tremendous impact he has had on my ideas and ways of doing research.

Sandy Wachholz, of the University of Southern Maine, has been colleague, friend, and sister. She is always there to spur me on, celebrate my successes, and believe in my ability to produce excellent academic work. We have been together since being in the 'gold-fish bowl' of temporary contracts. Our laughter and talk are always a tonic and inspire me to continue through thick and thin.

The study on which this book is based was funded by a grant from the Social Sciences and Humanities Research Council of Canada. My appointment as Canada Research Chair in Qualitative Research and Analysis has allowed me the time and financial support to bring this project to fruition.

Virgil Duff at University of Toronto Press has been encouraging since I first approached him with a proposal for this book. The anonymous reviewers for the press made constructive and useful suggestions that have surely improved the final text.

Last thanks go to my family. My parents have had an impact on everything I do that is too profound for words. My sister encouraged me to do better and think deeply. She is always with me.

My children, Lisa-Jo, Cheryl, and Jordan, have shared all my academic journeys with me. They were young children when I began studying sociology, and they have heard and participated in conversations about every project I have done. Now, as adults, they continue to take my breath away with their brilliance, creativity, and spirit of service.

Words fail when I try to encapsulate in a few sentences the place of my husband, Will C. van den Hoonaard, in my life both scholarly and personal. His faith in and encouragement of my work is unfailing and beyond anything anyone has a right to expect. We share all our ideas and benefit from our varied projects. In many ways, our research activities have become like a dance, and we love the dance.

PART ONE

Introduction

1 Introduction

When an older man's wife dies, he enters a foreign country, one which offers few images of what it means to be a widower. The images with which he might be familiar, those in popular culture, surely do not refer to him. In popular novels, television shows and movies, the widower is usually a young, or possibly middle-aged, man whose wife has often died violently, in an accident or by being murdered, or of cancer. In *How to Talk to a Widower* (Tropper 2007), the protagonist is a young widower of 29 whose wife has died in a plane crash, while in the television show *Monk*, the widower is an obsessive-compulsive, middle-aged man whose wife was killed when their car was rigged with a bomb. In the film *Sleepless in Seattle*, we see a young widower, who is devoted to his young son, as a romantic lead. In contrast, older widowers often appear as lost and unable to cope, as we see in movies like *About Schmidt* or some variant of *Grumpy.Old Men*.

By Himself: The Older Man's Experience of Widowhood is about how older men experience and talk about being widowers in real life. We know very little about these men, and virtually all research about men as widowers focuses solely on the grieving process. *By Himself*, in contrast, focuses on the social meaning of being a widower and how men describe their experiences in ways that serve to protect their sense of themselves as men.

When I tell people that I study older widowers, I get a very predictable reaction. The first thing people usually say is that men get married almost immediately after their wives die. The second remark sums up the belief that men cannot take care of themselves; they cannot cook or clean. Old widowers are perceived as a sad lot. Are these stereotypes based in reality? How do men understand and explain their experiences when their wives have died? The in-depth interviews that form the basis of *By Himself* provide answers to these questions and begin to address widowhood from the perspective of widowers.

Over thirty years ago, in her classic book, *The Future of Marriage*, Jessie Bernard (1973) pointed out that men and women have different experiences of marriage even when they seem to encounter the same objective situations. As a result, we know that we need to study the perceptions of both men and women in order to understand the similarities and differences in the way they experience marriage. The same can be said of the experience of the end of marriage through divorce (Kaufman and Uhlenberg 1998) as well as through widowhood. Nonetheless, as Anne Martin-Matthews, noted in 1991 and more recently in 2000, research on widowhood has focused almost entirely on the experience of women (1991; 2000). *By Himself* addresses this important omission and avoids the usual practice of using women as the yardstick for measuring the experience of widowhood.

I conducted open-ended interviews with twenty-six widowers over 60 years old between 2000 and 2002, nineteen men in a variety of urban and rural locations in one of Canada's Atlantic Provinces[1] and seven men who live in Florida, in condominium-type retirement communities. All but three of the interviews took place in the men's homes, and they ranged between forty-five minutes and two hours in length. The design of the interview guide was very open, encouraging the participants to frame their own stories in their own ways. Although I included some themes that had been important in *The Widowed Self: The Older Woman's Journey through Widowhood*, my earlier study of widows (van den Hoonaard 2001), I tried to avoid limiting the men's discussions to topics that were important to women. The men brought in issues that I had not anticipated and approached the interview situation in ways that surprised me.

Existing scholarly literature on men's experiences as widowers is small and focuses on two themes: Who has a harder time becoming widowed, men or women? And what are the psychological aspects of widowhood, particularly grieving? An example of the first theme is a classic article by Felix Berardo (1970). He suggested that men have a harder time being widowers because they are likely to suffer more social isolation than women. He also suggested that men find less gratification in learning to do the household chores, which their wives had likely done, than widows find in learning their husbands' chores.[2]

Berardo's analysis (1970), now almost 40 years old, was based on the assumption of traditional gender roles within marriage and, similar to much of the literature regarding widowhood, treats the widowed as passive and beset with almost insurmountable problems. His research design did not allow men to relate what in their experience matters most to them, nor did it tap into how widowers rebuild their lives or the creativity with which they may meet the challenges of this most profound life transition.

Other studies of men's experiences as widowers concentrate on psychological issues, predominantly grieving and the mourning process (Campbell and Silverman 1996). For men, this may mean focusing on issues of masculinity that lead to inexpressiveness or on traditional gender norms (Thompson 1997). Often it entails comparing their experience to that of women (Field et al. 1997; Feinson 1986; Gilbar and Dagan 1995). Similarly, in the area of aging, some subjects, for example, friendship (Adams 1994), sibling ties (Matthews 1994), and caregiving (Harris and Bichler 1997), have traditionally been seen as women's issues and, therefore, scholars have developed concepts that look at them from a woman's standpoint.

Research on divorce has also concentrated on women and children although some argue that older men are more at risk when divorced in old age (e.g., Goldscheider 1990). Silverman (1996: 5) suggests that the same has happened with widowhood: 'there is a female bias in the way we conceptualize how people should respond to grief.' For example, Nan Stevens (1995) in her study, 'Gender and Adaptation to Widowhood in Later Life,' comments that a shortcoming of her own research is her use of a list of needs originally developed for a study on widows alone to determine levels of adaptation for both men and women.

Research concerning men's experiences of widowhood has also ignored the social meaning of being a widower. Unlike women, men are not experiencing an 'expectable life event' (Martin-Matthews 1991) when their spouses die. They, therefore, may not have considered the possibility of being in such a situation. Because there are proportionally so few widowers, they have an atypical status, with few peers to assist in adjustment and socialization (Blau 1961; Kalish 1976). Even at age 85, almost 56 per cent of men remain married compared to 12 per cent of women (Statistics Canada 2006, cited in Matthews & Beaman 2007: 119). Nonetheless, although the percentage of men who become widowed may be small, there are over 300,000 widowers in Canada (Statistics

Canada 2007). We know very little about the issues that are important to the men who find themselves in this unusual situation.

Two notable exceptions to the reluctance to ask men directly about their experience as widowers are a British doctoral dissertation, *Gender, Age and Widowhood: How Older Widows and Widowers Differently Realign Their Lives*, by Kate Davidson (1999) and an American study, *Resilient Widowers: Older Men Speak for Themselves* (Moore and Stratton 2002). Davidson's work provides an intriguing look at the different meanings widowhood has for men and women. For example, while both experience 'loneliness,' widows are better at coping with 'aloneness' (108); and while women want a companion of the opposite sex to 'go out with,' men want one to 'come home to' (Davidson 2004). Alinde Moore and Dorothy Stratton (2002) interviewed 52 widowers in the United States about their experiences. Their study focuses on resilience. I had many occasions to consult their book while analyzing my own data, and the comparisons and contrasts complement my closer reading of the discourse the men used in the interview situation, often in an attempt to highlight their masculine selves.

In recent years, we have begun to see a few doctoral dissertations that explore some aspect of older or middle-aged men's experiences as widowers. The doctoral students interviewed men through groups and activities in which widowers generally do not participate. Ronin, for example, interviewed members of support groups to explore the creation of meaning (Ronin 2000), and Crummy spoke to Christian men, most of whom live in retirement communities, to study the resilience of widowers (Crummy 2002). These methods of recruitment may have been a result of the challenge involved in finding widowers to participate in the research, a frequent problem. They surely affected the findings, which may be as atypical as the men who participated in the studies.

This research differs from more traditional ways of studying widowhood. It keys into the importance of using symbolic interactionism in the presentation of empirical data and theoretical insights. How do answers grow directly from the inductive approach taken by symbolic interactionism?

Theoretical Foundations

By Himself: The Older Man's Experience of Widowhood sits on the foundation of symbolic interactionism – a way of looking at the world from the perspective of those being studied. As such, it not only explores how widowers described their relationships but also how they negoti-ated those relationships (Becker 1996). It recognizes that 'all terms are relational,' and that a trait, such as being a widower or an old man, is not simply a 'fact but rather an interpretation of that fact' (Becker 1998, 132, 134). Hence, symbolic interactionism and qualitative re-search are the most relevant approaches to use in order to understand this social process.

Howard S. Becker (1996) highlights three components of the epistem-ology of qualitative research, all of which find resonance in *By Himself*. First is the centrality of ascertaining the viewpoints of those studied. The in-depth interview style encourages participants to share their points of view. The questions in the interview guide[3] were as broad as possible to allow the participants to interpret and report on their ex-perience in their own way.

Becker's second point is the emphasis on everyday life and lived ex-perience. In-depth interviews encourage people to talk about what happened in their own words. Implicit in this approach is the recogni-tion that, in this case, widowers have an important understanding of their lives and can tell us about their own interpretation of events.

These first two points allow us to see older widowers' 'definition of the situation,' which has consequences for how they live their lives and interpret their place in the social world. They also provide an opportun-ity for us to avoid falling into the trap of seeing the experiences of wid-owers solely in terms of how they diverge from women's experiences.

Becker's third point is that ethnography provides a fuller description than variable analysis. This type of work is notable for its breadth. It elucidates a wide range of issues rather than studying relatively few variables. It sees widowers as multi-dimensional individuals who interact with other individuals, bureaucracies, and with themselves in order to understand their everyday lives.

Thus, the focus of *By Himself* is on meaning rather than on rates or measures (W.C. van den Hoonaard, 1997: 57). For example, rather than count how often the widowers see their children or friends, *By Himself* concentrates on how widowers talk about their relationships with their children and friends and their understanding of the meaning and na-ture of those relationships. Rather than look at how often the men par-ticipate in outside activities, *By Himself* looks at how the men talk about those activities and what they mean to them as widowers.

This approach seeks to understand social processes rather than offer causal explanations (W.C. van den Hoonaard 1997: 58). Instead of trying to understand only why widowers seem to remarry so frequently and quickly, we will examine how they interpret remarriage and how they understand and resolve challenging issues such as their desire not to mislead women who might interpret friendliness as romantic intention.

Symbolic interactionism also uses an inductive approach, one that draws theoretical insights along the way that help us to understand the data rather than to start with predetermined theoretical assumptions. In this way we do not allow those suppositions to define the case and thereby lose 'those aspects of our case that weren't in the description of the category we started with' (Becker 1998: 124). Had I used a limiting definition, for example, of who would be included in my sample of widowers, I would have lost the participation of the 30 per cent of the men who volunteered and were either married or in a permanent couple relationship. By remaining open to discovery during data collection, we can continuously add ideas to our collection of data – 'the essence of the [interactionist] method' (Becker 1996).

Anne Martin-Matthews, one of the first Canadian sociologists to study and write about widowhood, has pointed out, 'a symbolic interactionist approach is better able to ascertain the basis of responses to bereavement and widowhood and to account for factors that [other theoretical perspectives] cannot adequately consider' (1991: 9). It permits us to achieve some level of *Verstehen* (Weber 1949), the attempt to understand the world from the point of view of those studied (Fine 1990).

By Himself is organized so theoretical and conceptual insights interweave with the data they grow out of. This approach differs from the more conventional presentation of hypotheses, variables, concepts, and relevant literature appearing in advance of the data. Throughout, the reader will notice the continual presentation of both empirical data and theoretical insights. For example, in their description of the death of their wives, many widowers used language that focused on their contribution to the diagnosis of the final illness. The concept of 'agency speech' (Kirsi et al. 2000: 161) which focuses on the teller as an independent actor provides an understanding of the widowers' need to express having had some control over the process.

The book also uses the concept of the 'active interview' (Holstein and Gubrium 1995) in the analysis of not only what the widowers said, but how they said it. It sees the interview as a social encounter and goes beyond seeing 'subjects' simply as 'passive vessels of answers.' Rather, the widowers participated as individuals who situated both me and themselves in social positions through what they said and did during our interview encounter.

Social Context of the Research

The men who participated in this study lived in two places which present very different social contexts. Most lived in an Atlantic Province of Canada and the rest in retirement communities in Florida. They also represented different ethnic groups.

In Atlantic Canada, the participants were almost all of English, Scottish, or Irish background. One man was Acadian,[4] another came from a Jewish background, and one was from Southern Europe. This breakdown reflects the very homogeneous population of the Atlantic region of Canada. Although the provinces in this part of the country do contain small cities, they fit into the category of 'predominantly rural' because about 50 per cent of the population lives in rural communities (du Plessis, Beshiri, Bollman, & Clemenson 1996).

Residents explicitly differentiate between 'locals' and those 'from away.' In fact, to qualify as being a real local one must have been born in the region. It would be even better if one's grandparents were from the region, and the best one can be is a descendent of Loyalists. Most of the Canadian participants were locals.[5]

These widowers asserted their local pedigree during the interviews through pointing out connections with other local families and individuals. This practice allows people who qualify as locals to place one another socially. If a person knows who your father, mother, or cousin is, he or she knows a great deal about you. If people cannot place you, you are, by definition, from away, an outsider. It can be very difficult for those who have moved to the region from other places to make friends with real locals.

Being able to demonstrate one's local roots also helps a man to demonstrate his 'masculinity by proxy through the performance of localness' (Campbell 2006: 95). This effort was explicit in my interviews in Canada. The men frequently asked if I knew particular people or where specific places *used to* be. This practice allowed them to demonstrate their expertise in local knowledge and to mark themselves as locals. As Hugh Campbell (2006: 96) has noted, they became 'embedded in a sense of history that provide[d] the legitimizing power of tradition, thus stability, and therefore normalcy' through a display of their local origins.

Tradition, stability, and normalcy contribute to a strong sense of the region's having a very distinct way of life. Conversations frequently revolve around the idea of how much more friendly people are here compared to what it is like in big cities where 'you probably wouldn't even know your neighbour.' In the Atlantic region, everybody knows everybody else, and mutual helpfulness is the norm. The quality of life is, by definition, higher than in other regions of the country. This valorization of the region contributes to a conservatism which protects the way of life that people want to preserve. One cornerstone of the way of life is Tim Horton's coffee shop.[6]

Walk into any Tim Horton's at about 10:00 in the morning, and you will see a group of about ten older men sitting at adjacent tables. They will be wearing jeans and flannel shirts, drinking coffee, and 'shooting the breeze.' Occasionally, but not often, there might be one or two women at one of the tables. The men have arrived singly, but each knew his buddies would be there. Participation in these coffee groups is comparable to the pub culture that Hugh Campbell described in small-town New Zealand which he called 'pub(lic) masculinity' (2006: 95). Tim Horton's is such an iconic setting in Atlantic Canada that we might refer to 'Tim's masculinity' as one way that older men establish themselves as real locals, that is, real men.

The region has also escaped, particularly among older segments of the population, an emptying out of the churches. The parking lots of local churches are full on Sunday mornings, and many activities and organizations are church centred, especially in the more rural areas.

Even in the small urban areas, the province has a small-town feel, and those who have high-status careers – lawyers, professors, and doctors – dress in casual, rural clothes that allow them to blend in with those of more modest means or less education. For example, some years ago, two men were arranging to share the use of a small tractor, one to work in his orchard during the fall, the other to plow snow. The two men were dressed very casually and talked about local matters. A casual observer might have thought they were two farmers. It was only later that it became clear that both of them were professors at a local university. They had been using impression management (Goffman 1959) to appear to each other as local, rural men in order to claim legitimacy and masculinity.

Although most of the Canadian widowers had not been farmers or foresters, they did identify with the rural masculinity on a symbolic level (Brandth & Haugen 2005). Some identified themselves as 'outdoors kind of guys' while others employed 'props' or 'identity objects' such as skis, kayaks, and snowmobiles to project rural, masculine selves. Hunting, fishing, and other 'wilderness activities' form the core of rural men's traditional competencies, and the Atlantic Canadian men made use of these components to cement their masculine identities.

In Florida, however, the social context was entirely different. All of the men lived in condominium-type retirement communities in Southeast Florida. Commercial developers built these communities that have attracted retirees from big cities to the Sunbelt where they 'live like other people vacation' (van den Hoonaard 1992). There is a fairly large concentration of elderly Jews living in the retirement communities of South Florida, and the communities in which Jews live tend to be virtually all Jewish.

In these retirement communities,[7] residents generally own their apartments or houses and share the outside property including grass areas, the local streets, at least one swimming pool, clubhouse, and shuffleboard courts. Some communities also have a golf course. Homeowners' associations usually manage the common areas.

The symbolic and physical centre of the community is the pool and clubhouse area. Here formal events take place as well as informal social gatherings. Just as one would see groups of men at 'Tim's' at 10:00 in the morning in Atlantic Canada, one could tell time by observing which groups were sitting around the pool or in the clubhouse playing cards.

These immigrant retirees have brought their Jewish, northern culture with them. They do not make any attempt to meet socially or integrate with local Floridians. Restaurants, theatres, delis, and bagel shops have sprung up to meet their needs. For men, status and masculinity are claimed through previous occupational success, whether as small-business owners or professionals (Dunlop et al. 1997: 83), and through the accomplishments of children and grandchildren. Because most of the residents moved south when they retired, they usually do not have children living nearby.

Residents see their lives as relatively unstructured. Nonetheless, they do play cards at particular times, swim at particular times, and go out to restaurants for meals on a regular basis. The organization of their everyday lives creates and reinforces social as well as temporal boundaries within the community.

One boundary that is very clear is between married and widowed people. Widowers and widows both experience a loss of friends and often find themselves excluded from social groups. Much socializing takes place in couple groups, and there are few places where men gather on their own except on the golf course and at card games. This is particularly striking in the culture of eating out that characterizes retirement-community life. Women often go to restaurants in groups (travelling together unlike the men at Tim's who arrive one by one) while men rarely do (van den Hoonaard 1994).

The heart of my research consisted of in-depth interviews. The next few pages discuss how I designed the interviews and the process of interviewing. As we will see, the men's strategies during the interviews reflected the social contexts as well as their sense of themselves as men.

The Interviews

There were two things I, as a sociologist, wanted to accomplish through the interviews. The first was to interview a group of men over 60 who had experienced widowhood within the previous ten years, and who lived in a variety of areas in a province in Atlantic Canada. Second, I wanted to avoid limiting my research to themes that I had found to be significant to older widows whom I had interviewed for an earlier book (van den Hoonaard 2001).

I started by interviewing three widowers in Florida in order to try out my interview guide and sensitize myself to men's approaches to losing their wives. I found these men through contacts whom I had met when I had carried out a study of life in a Florida retirement community. I had known one widower most of my life, while friends and relatives made the initial contact with the others. Based on these early interviews, two of which took place over the telephone, I revised my interview guide and was ready to look for participants in Atlantic Canada. At a later stage of the research, I returned to Florida and interviewed four more men.

I knew that recruiting participants might be the most challenging aspect of the project (see Wister and Strain 1986). Because there are so few widowers, and men do not volunteer to participate in research as much as women, I used several methods of recruitment. Contacts in seniors' organizations as well as individual friends helped me locate and recruit widowers. As well, I used local media, including newspapers, radio, and television, in publicizing the research, a strategy that had been very successful in my earlier book about widows. I also tried using a snowball technique, but this method is not as successful when seeking male research participants as it is with women (Davidson 1999). In short, I cast as wide a net as possible to find men who fit the criteria of the research and were willing to participate.

As I had anticipated, widowers were not easy to find. A number of friends who knew men who fit the criteria offered to approach them on my behalf, and some of those men did participate in the study. These participants may have been doing favours for their friends and tended to be more reserved and reticent than the men who volunteered in response to publicity about the book (Doucet 2007).

Most of the participants responded to a variety of articles and stories covered in the local media. The media were more than happy to call attention to the research. Journalists began calling me as soon as the project was publicized by my university. In fact, when I emailed a province-wide radio show, *Mainstreet*, on CBC in September, 2001 and suggested that its listeners might be interested in my work, I was interviewed on the show that very afternoon.

When I asked the men what made them volunteer, many of them said that they could see that I needed help and that they figured that my work would be legitimate because I had already written a book about widows. Interestingly, when I appeared on a Cable Ten show on television and noted that I only needed a few more men to complete the research for a book, I did not get a single volunteer. My guess is that men may not have felt that I needed their help and, therefore, did not reply.

Confidentiality of participants in this type of book is always a paramount concern. It is particularly challenging in an area with a small, relatively stable population, in which people have many interconnections. To protect the men's identities, I have changed their and their wives' names. I have also altered some details of their stories and descriptions of the places in which they live to prevent individual identification. It is for this reason that I do not include case studies or details about the widowers. Attempts to disguise the widowers through changing some details may not be successful in this small area.[8]

I had not initially intended to interview in Florida a second time. However, the men in Atlantic Canada were so reserved, as well as hard to find, that I returned to Florida and interviewed four more men (for a total of seven). The Florida sample is somewhat older than the Atlantic Canadian sample, ranging in age from 75 to 87 years old with an average age of 81. The addition of the group in Florida provided the book with some cultural and religious diversity – an unanticipated strength – which enriched the analysis because Atlantic Canada is both homogeneous and primarily rural.

I interviewed most of the men in their homes and always at a time convenient for them. We sat where the men chose, usually in the living room or, occasionally, at a kitchen table or, in the case of Florida, on a patio. One man insisted that I interview him at my office (which I happily obliged), and I interviewed three men in Florida over the telephone. With the permission of the participants, I taped all the interviews and transcribed each in full. Most of the men maintained a business-like demeanour, and most did not offer coffee or tea. The interviews with the men lasted one hour on average with a range of forty-five minutes to three hours.

The length of the interviews depended on each participant's willingness to answer the prompting questions in an expansive manner. My strategy was to understate my professional status although some men said that they had volunteered to participate (at least partly) because I had credibility as a published author and was, therefore, not a neophyte. Understating my status when interviewing older widowers may have elicited the didactic tone some men used in the interviews. Nonetheless, my being a younger woman (50) encouraged some men to treat me like a daughter and resulted in their manifesting their usual demeanour when interacting with women. The behaviour included taking charge of the interview and using a variety of strategies to reinforce their masculinity (see van den Hoonaard 2009a).

The two groups of widowers experienced quite different social contexts, and, in some ways, the men's understanding of their experiences reflect these differences. Nonetheless, they all lived most of their adult lives in the second half of the twentieth century, and all encountered highly valued components of masculinity that included independence, autonomy, stoicism, power, and control.[9] Therefore, there are also striking similarities in the way the men talked about their experiences.

Analysis of the Data

It became apparent in my study that the widowers[10] had been working very hard to make sure that I understood that they were still men. The men's style of interaction claimed and reinforced an air of masculinity. Every topic is saturated with these widowers' efforts to portray themselves as 'real' men. This effort was most obvious in the men's discussions around housework and cooking, two traditional feminine tasks, and in attitudes towards remarriage. I had no choice but to approach the data using the lens of masculinity. The men's style of interaction was 'an act of gender signification that crie[d] out for analysis' (Schwalbe and Wolkomir 2001: 211).

I became convinced that these older widowers were reacting to precariousness in their identities as men by using impression management (Goffman 1959) to reinforce their sense of masculinity. I therefore went back to the tapes of the interviews to listen to them once again to make sure I was right that the participants were, indeed, 'doing gender' (West and Zimmerman 1987) throughout the interviews. I came away more assured that I was correct in my interpretation. The men's tones of voice – whether didactic, aggressive, or affectionate – were those of dominant men talking to a subordinate, younger woman.

The interview situation, in which these men found themselves, presented what David H. J. Morgan (1992: 100) might refer to as 'a paradigmatic example of masculinity under challenge' because they were widowed, retired, might become emotional, were being interviewed by a woman, and were older. As Calasanti and King (2005: 7) have pointed out, 'our constructions of old age contain no positive content.' The situation elicited a particularly forceful effort on the part of the interview participants to establish themselves as men.

The widowers' task was a difficult one, for there is no available, familiar image of being an old man and a widower that men can adopt in their presentation of self and still portray themselves as masculine. They were forced to use the symbols and practices that are borrowed from a repertoire that they had learned in their youth (Spector-Mersel 2006).

Because the men were so uncertain about their identity as widowers and the connotations of being a widower, I began to question the images of widowers that are available in contemporary society. There are a large number of widowers who appear as characters on television or in the movies, often middle-aged or young men whose wives have died tragically. There are also many novels in which the main character is a widower. In these novels, as well, many of the widowers are youngish men whose wives have died violently, either as a result of murder or an accident. Stephen King's *Bag of Bones* (1998) provides an example.

For this book, I attempted to understand the experience of the participants as deeply as possible and to see the world through their eyes. The gender and age differences made such a high standard of empathy recede into the distance as I continued analysing the interviews using a thematic approach. Thus, the analysis of the stories the men told and the way they told those stories have become the heart of this book. Through their narratives, we can see what it was the men felt important to communicate about their experiences coupled with the challenge of maintaining a desired self-identity in a situation that does not provide many positive images which they could use in the process.

By Himself next looks closely at the various threads that make up an older widower's life as well as how he talks about them. Chapter Two explicates more deeply the challenges of masculinity for older men and the impact they had on the how the participants talked about their experiences. Chapter Three discusses how the men talked about their wives' illnesses and deaths. Chapter Four accompanies the men on their first steps as widowers, when they planned their wives' funerals and did the necessary paperwork.

Chapters Five through Seven focus on the efforts of the widowers to negotiate relationships with their children, with women, and with friends. The old ways of interacting did not work as well and became fraught with unknown pitfalls that they might not have anticipated. Their wives had often been the intermediaries between them and their children, and negotiating their new relationship elicited ambivalent feelings that they had not expected. Deciding whether or not to develop a new romantic relationship was a central concern, while desiring control over the process and fearing misinterpretation dominated their relationships with women. Some friends deserted the men, and they often felt uncomfortable in the company of couples.

Chapters Eight and Nine discuss the men's everyday lives. Chapter Eight looks at how the widowers said they spent their time. The widowers found it imperative to spend as little time as possible in their houses alone, and they explained the importance of 'getting out' at the same time as they described a round of activities that appear to be spontaneous and to require a minimum of ongoing commitment.

Chapter Nine focuses on the two activities that encompassed the biggest challenge to older widowers' sense of themselves as men: cooking and housekeeping. It is in talking about these components of 'women's work' that the men confronted chores with which they often had had no experience and that are strongly identified with women. In response, the men emphasized the simplicity of their cooking and their having lower standards of house cleaning than their wives had had.

Finally, Chapter Ten summarizes the major facets of men's lives as widowers and places these findings in the context of what we already knew about older men's lives. It is my hope that this book will provide a deeper understanding of widowers' lives as they see them, with all the complexity and diversity that they entail.

2 Masculinity and Older Widowers

One of the first revelations of my research was the extent to which older widowers leaned on reinforcing their masculinity when they talked about their experiences as widowers both in what they said and how they approached the interview situation.

The interviews initially began with the same opening question that I had used in *The Widowed Self: The Older Woman's Journey through Widowhood* (van den Hoonaard 2001). I designed them to encourage the participants to decide what aspects of being widowed were most important to them and to elaborate on the issues about which they talked:

> What I would like for you to do now is tell me your experience with being a widower. You can start where you want and end where you want. I'm just interested in finding out about your experience.

This question had been very effective when I was talking to widows, but was quite ineffective when I used it in the interviews with widowers. It quickly became obvious that the men were not going to let me get through the entire question. They simply started talking over that first question, and I soon shortened it to: 'What's it like being a widower?' Or, 'Tell me about being a widower.' Interestingly, in response to this question, many men talked about their experiences with women and their willingness or unwillingness to remarry.

This focus on the possibility of developing a connection with a new woman came as a surprise. It alerted me to the idea that the issue of re-partnering is a top-of-mind issue for many widowers. As the analysis continued, it became more and more obvious that even for men who did not want to remarry, developing a relationship with a new woman was

an intrinsic part of being widowed for these men. Virtually every participant brought up this topic before I had a chance to ask about it directly.

In addition, the men had emphasized their masculinity in their responses to questions on just about every topic. When discussing cooking and housework, for example, many described these tasks in ways
that protected their sense of masculinity and ensured that I understood
that they were still men even though they had become competent at
chores traditionally thought of as women's work.

The strength of the impression management the men were using to
emphasize their masculinity led me to query literature on masculinity
to understand the participants' approach. Erving Goffman, noted for
his perceptiveness in observing and interpreting the details of everyday life, provided an early description of what would come to be called
hegemonic masculinity (Connell 1987): 'In an important sense, there is
only one complete unblushing male in America: a young, married,
white, urban, northern, heterosexual Protestant father of college education, fully employed, of good complexion, weight and height, and a
recent record in sports' (Goffman 1963: 128). He understood that all
(North) American men encountered the world from this perspective.
Goffman suggested that all men know how close or far they are from
this 'unblushing' standard of hegemonic masculinity, of being a 'proper
man.' Forty years later, this standard remains the same.

Hegemonic masculinity (Connell 1987) is an ideal type, however, that
the vast majority of men never accomplish. In addition, there are many
dominant and subordinate masculinities that vary historically, culturally, and among men with a variety of social locations, not the least of
which are age and marital status. The highly valued masculine attributes that old, widowed men face in their attempt to maintain a manly
identity include, among others, 'manifesting power and control'
(Spector-Mercel 2006, Slevin 2008, Coles 2008, Charmaz 1994, Meadows
& Davidson 2006, Moss, Moss, Kilbride, & Rubinstein 2007); 'being independent and self-reliant' (Aléx et al. 2008, Gross & Blundo 2005,
Gershick & Miller 1995, Ribeiro, Paúl, & Nogueira 2007, Moss et al.
2007); 'exhibiting stoicism' (Courtney 2000b, Calasanti 2004, Drummond
& Smith 2006); 'self-control' (Calasanti 2004, Meadows & Davidson
2006); 'heterosexuality' (Slevin 2008, Coles 2008, Aléx et al. 2008, Loe
2004, Connell 1987, Meadows & Davidson 2006, Bennett 2007); 'youthful
appearance and embodiment' (Slevin 2008) 'objectification of women'
(Coles 2008); 'achievement in the work world' (Spector-Mercel 2006,

Calasanti & King 2005, Calasanti 2004, Bernard ([1981] 1995), Meadows & Davidson 2006, Bennett 2007); 'a high level of education' (Aléx et al. 2008); 'technical competence' (Henson & Rogers 2001); 'scientific attitude' (Rubin 2004); and 'being in the male center' (Aléx et al. 2008, Edley & Wetherell 1995). Fundamentally, what all these components have in common is that they describe a person who is not feminine, i.e., who does not share personal characteristics or ways of doing things that we associate with women (Campbell & Carroll 2007, Courtney 2000a, Edley & Wetherell 1995, Ducat 2004, Calasanti 2003).

There is very little scholarship on old men *as men* (for exceptions see Calasanti 2004, Calasanti and King 2005, and van den Hoonaard 2007). This modest level of research deals mainly with men's understanding of their bodies and health problems (e.g. Drummond and Smith 2006). As Edward Thompson, Jr. (2006) has noted, the study of aging and masculinity is in its infancy. Gabriela Spector-Mersel (2006) has identified the absence of 'cultural guidelines' for how to be both an old man and a real man. *By Himself* extends the discussion by looking at widowers, who not only have a status normally held by women but also are not in a relationship with a woman. What do we know about older widowers and masculinity?

Older Widowers and Masculinity

There is almost no one who has written on the topic of older widowers and masculinity. An exception is Kate Bennett (2007) who has used Robert Brannon's classic four themes of masculinity (1976): 'no sissy stuff; the sturdy oak; the big wheel; and give 'em hell,' as a framework. In '"No Sissy Stuff": Towards a Theory of Masculinity and Emotional Expression in Older Widowed Men,' she notes that the strong emotions associated with bereavement challenge men to live up to the masculine ideal and thereby increase the gap between that ideal and their lived reality. Bennett also discovered an unanticipated discourse in her study of widowers regarding explicit statements or thoughts about making decisions to continue on with their lives. She suggests that these statements reflect themes of: 'carelessness of life and the decision to live, stoicism, affective and behaviourial associations, and mortality' (Bennett 2005: 147). Although the widowers I spoke to did not raise this issue explicitly, the control they exhibited over their lives encompasses stoicism and decision-making about how to live their lives.

Old widowers may find it particularly difficult to achieve many components of the 'unblushing' standard of masculinity that Goffman described. They have lost the ability to claim an authentic youthful appearance and, normally, participation in the work world simply by virtue of how many years they have lived. They have also strayed from the standards of being married and, therefore, visible heterosexuality. It should be noted inter alia, that the absence of these characteristics confirms ageist stereotypes, but are contrary to the fact that people become more diverse as they get older (Binstock 1985). The societal view of old people is that they are homogeneous. Although we may argue that the gendered characteristics of being a man are socially constructed, the societal belief is that they are essential, innate characteristics. The old widowers to whom I spoke often accepted essentialist ideas about masculinity. They found themselves in the unenviable position of having to find ways of claiming their masculinity.

Even in the interview situation, itself, the challenge remained for these widowers to live up to the standards of being a real man both because they gave up some control by agreeing to be interviewed and because they were discussing a situation in which they were relatively powerless about which they might have become emotional.

Thus, as the book progresses, we can see many instances in which the men worked to accomplish masculinity through 'doing gender' (West and Zimmerman 1987) and impression management (Goffman 1959). The concept of 'mosaic masculinities' (Coles 2008) identifies and highlights the ways these widowers claimed masculinity in the different aspects of their lives. This concept suggests that men who find themselves far from the hegemonic ideal of masculinity may negotiate a masculine self through: 'drawing on fragments or pieces of hegemonic masculinity which they have the capacity to perform and piecing them together ... to come up with their own standard of masculinity' (Coles 2008: 237–8). The participants developed a 'coherent pattern' of themselves as men. For example, they took the stance of an objective observer of their wives' illnesses and deaths to associate themselves with masculinity even though they were in a situation over which they had minimal control. By telling the story of their wives' deaths with little emotion, the men were able to demonstrate their stoicism, a basic component of masculinity.

There is no positive image of old widowers available, and the negative images that do exist paint a picture of widowers as passive and socially marginal. Many men are reluctant to identify with this unattractive status. The next section of this chapter illustrates how ageism and issues of masculinity result in widower as a weak identity.

Widower: A Weak Identity

Literary portrayals of widowers diverge from popular images, as the excerpts from Alice Munro and David Bottoms in the epigraphs show. These characters are disconnected from society. They are men who live in the past with little 'ornament' or 'sentiment.' Widowers are not likely to find either of these representations very attractive when they think about what being a widower means to them. Caught between the romantic image of the young widower and the image of the old, bewildered widower, older men have no satisfactory role to adopt. Some widowers, in response to this conundrum, responded by using 'identity work' (Snow & Anderson 1987: 1348) to distance themselves from the negative connotations of being widowers. In other words, they attempted to create 'personal identities' that were more congruent with their self-conception than the sad, bewildered individuals implied by images of old widowers.

In addition, because there are comparatively few widowers, they are relatively rare and 'exotic.' I first noticed this situation when my university announced that I had received a grant to study widowers. There was immediate media attention at a level I certainly did not experience for my studies of older widows. I also discovered that many people are not sure what to call men whose wives have died – some people I encountered referred to them as 'male widows' while others made jokes about how quickly widowers vanish into remarriage. There seemed to be no clear picture of men after they became widowed.

In fact, the very meaning and identity of being a widower are fuzzy for the participants of this study. Unlike widows, who described a definite instant, an 'identifying moment' (Charmaz 1991; van den Hoonaard 2001), in which they suddenly understood that they were widows, that their identity had changed, the widowers demonstrated the vagueness of their identity as widowers. They expressed an uncertainty about when people first referred to them as widowers or even if they had ever thought of themselves as widowers.[1] They did not know where they belonged in the foreign country which they had entered when their wives died.

Some of the men I interviewed did not seem entirely clear as to what to call themselves either. The identity of widower does not have definite characteristics. It is almost empty of content and, therefore, has a weak hold on its incumbents. It is, therefore, a weak identity.

Contributing to this popular and muddled view of widowers is the fact that about one-third of the men who volunteered for this study had remarried or were in a permanent, couple relationship. In contrast, none of the volunteers for my study about older widows had remarried. This raised the question: why did men who had remarried not disqualify themselves from the study while women did? How strong was the widower identity in these men's self-concept? As the next few pages show, becoming a widower is not something that men expect to experience, and 'widower' is often a very weak identity, one that many men find possible to reject.

For men, becoming widowed is definitely *not* an 'expectable event' (Martin-Matthews 1991). In fact, when I asked participants if there was anything that surprised them about their experiences with being widowers, seven explicitly answered that simply the fact of being widowed was the most surprising. For example, one man observed:

> No [surprises] ... Because I *never* thought about it ... You know, my wife, it was a standing thing that I was going to die a long, long time before her ... It *never* entered my head, or I *never* even thought about what I was going to have to do when I was alone ... No plans, I *never* dreamed that ... I *never* even thought about what it would be like ... That wasn't a part of what was supposed to happen. [emphasis added] (Chad)[2]

Like Alinde Moore and Dorothy Stratton (2002: 89), I found that husbands assumed that they would die first and that, unlike for women, there may be no 'on time' loss of their wives. Even men whose wives were ill for some time before they died had still believed that, somehow, they would die first. The repetition of the word, 'never,' in the quotation above underlines the complete lack of anticipation of becoming a widower for this man. Chad and other widowers had not imagined in their wildest dreams that they might find themselves in the position of being a widower. This unexpectedness contributes in important ways to many men's uncertainty about how to relate to themselves as widowers.

As unlikely as it may seem, some participants did not consider themselves widowers. Two simply stated that they did not think of themselves as widowers. Others' comments demonstrated a definite vagueness in their understanding of their identity. For example, in response to my query about whether he thinks of himself as a widower, Leroy responded:

> Uh, well, I know I'm that way, but I guess I don't think of it that way ... I don't get any hangups on that. That's just part of life, you know.

Two men felt more comfortable thinking of themselves as bachelors:

> Well, I say I consider myself a widower. Functionally, I don't consider myself a widower ... I don't consider [widowhood] as something I have to adapt to. Maybe bachelorhood would be better. I simply see myself as a free agent and do what I please when I want to do it ... Maybe as a bachelor rather than a widower ... I'm not functioning any differently than if I were a bachelor, let's put it that way. So, I don't know where being a widower is relevant. (George)

A man who had become widowed in his 50s recounted his trouble with figuring out what to call himself. His sense of dislocation was profound. He talked about the awkwardness of deciding which box to tick off on a form that asked about marital status:

> Like, you fill out these forms, and you have to check off single, divorced, widowed, whatever. And so, for a time, I wasn't sure what I was. Like I'd check off widower, but that didn't feel right. Single didn't feel right. It ... felt to me like I didn't fit in any of those categories ... It was more than when I was confronted with forms that I needed to check off. It just felt like none of those blanks felt right to me. They didn't fit any more. (Leonard)

Rather than describing this situation as confusing, women often explain that filling out forms provided the identifying moment when they realized that their status had shifted from wife to widow (van den Hoonaard 1997).

Kate Davidson (1999: 169) suggests a possible explanation for these men's uncertainty about whether being widowed entailed their acquiring a new identity, that of widower. She noted that 'when a husband loses a wife, he loses a person, but not a status.' Women, on the other hand, whose marital status is central to their identity, not only lose a person but also a status upon their husband's death.[3]

By resisting the adoption of the term widower to refer to themselves, the men, especially those who chose to call themselves bachelors, were using our conversation to categorize themselves as something other than the lonely, lost men portrayed in the literature cited above. As Hollander and Gordon (2006: 190) have observed, '... in the case of *self-categorization* ... we make claims about ourselves as particular types of people' [emphasis in original]. In Goffman's terms, the use of the word bachelor served as a tool of impression management (1959) and preserved the men's identities as (hetero)sexual and, thereby, allowed them to retain their status as men (Calasanti 2004). It made it possible for them to distance themselves from the characteristics they associated with being old widowers. They were, therefore, able to claim personal identities associated with youth, virility, and freedom rather than with the social role of 'widower' which confers a lower status on its incumbents. As we shall see throughout this book, the men often made strong cases for the type of people they were, masculine, effective men.

Compounding these two interpretations, terms to refer to people who have lost their spouses reflect the dominant view of widowhood as a woman's experience. Widow is one of the few English words in which the root refers to the feminine rather than the masculine form. The word 'widow' originated from the Sanskrit meaning 'lonely, solitary' and was used before the year 900 AD. 'Widower,' however, first appeared in print around 1362 (Harper 2007). Usage of these two words reflects the different connotations of being widows and widowers. For example, it is quite common to hear a woman referred to as John's widow, but the converse, Mary's widower, sounds awkward. Similarly, a woman may become widowed, but a man does not become widowered.

The loss of status for women is so pronounced that they are often able to report exactly where they were and when they first thought of themselves as widows or when someone referred to them as widows. The men who participated in this study, in contrast, did not always remember or claimed not to care about being called a widower.

Although I was eager to avoid looking at men's experiences in comparison to those of women, widows' reports of an 'identifying moment' (Charmaz 1991) were so strong in both my study of widows' published autobiographical accounts (van den Hoonaard 1997) and my interview study with older widows (van den Hoonaard 2001) that I asked most of the widowers about this phenomenon.[4] Seven men stated outright that they did not remember the occasion when someone first called them widowers while five stated that they did. Four participants said that no one had used the term widower to refer to them, two clarifying that since they had not met any new people, there was no reason for anyone to call them a widower.

A few men remarked that they became aware that they were widowers because women immediately became interested in them:

> [Do you remember the first time that somebody referred to you as a widower or that you thought of yourself as a widower?] Oh my, well, I'll tell you what, the available female population soon let you know ... that you are available ... Suddenly they pay so much more attention to you ... It didn't take them long to let me know ... [5] (Marc)

As we shall see, the widowers interpreted any attention they received from women as motivated by women's seeing them as potential romantic partners.

Unlike widows, who report having a strong reaction to hearing themselves referred to as widows and use evocative words like 'shock,' 'it hit me,' 'made me feel sick to my stomach,' most men did not have a strong response to the word. In fact, most of the men said that they did not have any particular image that came to mind when they thought of the word widower. One man, who said that he 'knew damn well' that he was a widower, described a widower as 'just someone who's lost his wife. Period.' Thus, the men, while claiming not to care about the word widower, attempted to eliminate the status entirely. They rejected the social identity of widower.

From the quotations above, one might get the impression that the term widower does not conjure up an image for most men. However, scattered through the interviews are stereotypes and connotations of widowers. These cluster around the idea of widowers as lonely, old, and lost. As well, the men observed that widowers are rare. In these descriptions, it is clear that the participants were not describing themselves. Rather they used the contrast in order to demonstrate how well they were doing in adapting to their new life situation as well as to make a distinction between the demeaning aspects of the role-based social identity of widower and their own self-conception as competent men (Snow & Anderson 1987).

At the simplest level, some men simply saw a widower as a 'single person' who is 'living alone.' He is 'an old man' whom others may perceive as a 'lonely, old widower' with no 'spring in my step.' Some men seemed to agree with Alice Munro's vision that a widower is in danger of being 'useless, lazy, lost,' and someone who might 'sit and dwell.'

One Florida widower suggested that 'the average male becomes a female' (Jacob) when his wife dies while another used the term 'old maids' to refer to widowers other than himself. When I asked him for clarification, he remarked that most widowers either quickly find another woman or 'sit and die.' These images convey the message that some men do not cope very well. By contrasting themselves positively, the men claimed their masculinity as dominant, within the subordinate field of masculinity of older widowers, compared to others who were not able to be as strong in the face of widowhood as they.

Both widows and widowers believe that women are stronger and cope better than men when widowed (Davidson 1999: 111). Winston, who had been widowed twice, explained that women do better than men at rebuilding their lives. He believed that men were better in life-threatening emergencies, for example:

> Men might be better at surviving if, uh, say, they're thrown in a boat, in the middle of the ocean. And they're not going to be rescued and they've got to get somewhere ... if something happens and they're in the mountains, and they got to get out, but, in ordinary life, it seems to be that women are better.

He felt that women would be less likely to 'give in' when faced with widowhood than men. At the same time, he used stereotypical images of heroic masculinity to characterize men's, and by implication his, ability to cope in emergencies.

Finally, some men conveyed the image of being a widower as exotic, in an almost anomic position. They used terms like oddball, free agent, and rare breed to describe their status as widowers. Herbert described himself as an 'oddity' in his widowhood support group, whose female members 'make a little bit of a pet out of me.' Marc conveyed the aura of the widower as slightly dangerous when he referred to himself as a 'lone wolf.' The presumed 'desperation' of widowers to remarry because of their inability to take care of themselves (i.e., cook and do housework) may contribute to this sense of danger.

Matthew, who had moved from a rural area to a city about one year after his wife died, suggested that the image of the widower was different in each of the places: in the rural area, a widower joined the Seniors' Club and spent all his time playing cards in an explicitly 'feminine space' (Meadows & Davidson 2006). In the small city to which he had relocated, a widower like him was an 'elder bachelor.'

These varied and vague strands begin to address what it means to an older man to be a widower. He may be unsure of whether his identity is affected by the loss of his wife, although there were a few widowers who did talk about losing part of themselves and the difficulty of learning to talk about 'I' rather than 'we.' Most do not recall an identifying moment and cannot or will not communicate an image of widowers except in contrast to their own experiences.

These widowers do not have a strong sense of the social meaning of being a widower and reject what connotations they do admit to being aware of. They reject the possibility of a definite identity change or change in self-concept. The ability to distance oneself from the identity of widower, as well as claim uncertainty about their identity, reflects the unexpectedness of becoming a widower, the association of widowhood with women, and the invisibility of widowers.

Women are much more likely both to become and to remain widowed than men (Martin-Matthews 1991, Moore & Stratton 2002)). Thus, women are very aware that they may become widows; they recognize, incorporate, and rehearse the potential situation. Men, because they do not expect to be widowers, do not participate in this anticipatory socialization. In addition, men do not base their identity on their role as a husband (Martin-Matthews 1991: 64-5).

The combination of the numerical dominance of women (Martin-Matthews 1991; Moore & Stratton 2002) and widowers' likelihood of remarriage results in our associating widowhood exclusively with women. As a result, widowhood itself has become a feminized space (Meadows & Davidson 2006) with which men avoid identifying as a strategy to maintain a masculine self. Hence, some widowers refer to themselves as bachelors or similar to bachelors.

Gabriela Spector-Mersel (2006: 68) notes that there is at present: 'an absence of cultural guidelines for being both a "true" man and an aging person [and that this results in a] context in which contemporary older men struggle to build acceptable identities.' This struggle is likely exacerbated for widowers who not only lack the physical prowess and participation in paid work that are necessary to maintain a masculine identity but also are not in a relationship with a woman. They are experiencing widowhood, which is usually associated with a lack of control and a display of emotion that are decidedly unmanly in Western culture. The widowers used impression management both as interview participants and in thinking about themselves to establish selves as true men and 'construct legitimate personal identities'

(Spector-Mersel 2006: 78), using symbols of youth and middle age because there are no usable images of masculinity for older men.

Widowers are, thus, invisible in the social sphere of widowhood. Scholars assume they are 'rare' (Moore and Stratton 2002: 2). The phenomenon of older widowers was invisible even to Edward H. Thompson, who was one of the first to write about the absence of research on old men as men. Thompson (1994, quoted in Moore & Stratton 2002: 4) suggested that old men do not have to rebuild their lives and 'go it alone' after the death of a spouse.

Widowers are socially invisible, even to themselves. Moore and Stratton (2002: 4) suggest two reasons for this invisibility: first, that widowers' 'identity is masked by remarriage' and, second, that they do not socialize with each other in the same way that widows do.

Chapter Three looks at how men talked about their wives' deaths. It begins with the discovery that their wives were dying and uses a discourse-analytic approach to interpret how the men situated themselves as men within their stories.

PART TWO

Experiencing the Unexpected

3 Becoming a Widower

The first intimation that most of the men had that they might become widowers was when their wives received a diagnosis of a terminal or potentially terminal illness. Their descriptions of the onset of their wives' symptoms and the diagnosis are detailed and communicate the enormity of the event. The narratives lead up to the point of terminal diagnosis and the inevitable progression of the illness, which many summarized as 'all downhill.'

When the widowers talked about their wives' illnesses, they characterized the care they gave their wives as primarily comprising traditionally male tasks, such as renovating a room, rather than as personal care. They also communicated their admiration for the way their wives handled being ill and what their wives did to protect them from overwork, as well as what happened at the point when their wives died.

In looking at how the men talked about their wives' illnesses and deaths, I am using a discourse-analytic approach. The participants told stories that had definite plot lines, which they used to situate themselves as husbands, caregivers, and men. They recounted the discovery of their wives' impending deaths and their own place in the process using the same four modes of speech – factual, familistic, destiny, and agency speech – identified by Kirsi et al. (2000) in their study of men's written stories of caring for their wives. The use of these modes enabled the men to emphasize their masculinity as they told the story of their wives' illnesses and deaths.

In the first mode, 'factual speech,' the speaker provides: 'objective and neutral information about the facts and events of his wife's disease, he speaks with the vocabulary of the factual speech repertoire. In factual speech, the writer adopts the identity of an observer and reporter of the patient's [illness]' (156). Factual speech allowed the widowers to maintain a relatively unemotional demeanour. The participants who used this mode of speech often included causal arguments or descriptions and medical vocabulary (157).

Some men used a familistic speech repertoire that entailed focusing on their 'obligations as a family member and [their] commitment to [their] wives.' In using familistic speech, widowers claimed the identity of a responsible husband (157–8) and explained what they did during their wives' illnesses as a component of their marital role: 'I did what I had to do.' The participants, in using familistic speech, compared themselves favourably to men whose dedication was not as evident. For example, one man suggested that he spent more time visiting his wife at the hospital than most men would.

In the third mode, 'agentic speech, the [widower] adopt[ed] the identity of an independent actor' (161). He took centre stage in the telling of how his wife died. For example, several men emphasized the roles they took in encouraging their wives to see a doctor or in persuading the doctor to do more tests when they thought the diagnosis was not complete. Agentic speech was evident throughout many of the interviews. Thus, most of the men talked a great deal about their former occupations, titles and accomplishments in many places in the interviews. In doing so, they demonstrated their agency by 'staking out' (162) their lifelong accomplishments as men. The things they did while their wives were ill were consistent with their identities as agentic men.

When participants gave the impression that they were 'at the mercy of forces that [were] beyond [their] control' (163), they were using the vocabulary of 'destiny speech.' Widowers who used destiny speech characterized themselves as victims or the deaths of their wives as inevitable. Few participants used this strategy as an overall approach to the interview. Nonetheless, many used destiny speech to depict the progression of their wives' illnesses after diagnosis as 'all downhill from there.'

Diagnosis: And It Was Downhill from There

Many of the men used a 'factual speech repertoire' to talk about their wives' diagnoses and illnesses, particularly those whose wives died of cancer. They reported symptoms, tests, and meetings with doctors in a dispassionate and detailed manner. In these cases, the widowers started their discussion with a detailed, sometimes explicit, description of symptoms and the process of diagnosis of their illnesses. They often included exact dates for events such as surgery or the diagnosis.

Some men explained that their wives had been treating themselves for a thought-to-be minor ailment while others described a route to finding out how sick their wives were that included misdiagnoses or misplaced optimistic prognoses. Leroy's wife, for example, had been self-treating something that was, according to Leroy, 'growing like a grape.' He did not say how long she had been self-treating, but did remark, 'I used to see her putting cream on it,' because she initially thought it was a pimple. When she finally went to see her gynecologist, he said, 'Gees, I don't know what the heck that is,' and sent her to Halifax, a drive of several hours, for diagnosis. The doctors there informed Leroy that she had an aggressive cancer and 'won't be living by Christmas.'

Winston's wife had started to cough 'quite a bit ... coming from right inside her chest there,' although she did not have any pain. He was quite worried, but she told him that she had 'no pain or problems.' When she finally did go to the doctor, he thought she had an allergy. Finally, as Winston explained:

> He sent her for X-rays then she had some other tests ... And then she started to develop a headache.

The tests had revealed a spot on his wife's lung, but Winston thought the cancer had spread because his wife had previously been able to handle headache pain and this time the pain was obviously different. Finally, other tests showed much more extensive tumours in both lungs as well as her brain. The prognosis was that she had six months to live at the most. Winston's wife said that she would survive for only three months, and 'she was right.'

In contrast, Stan's wife died 'suddenly' of heart failure. But even he spoke of symptoms that he had not paid attention to because his wife had had polio as a child. He suspected that his wife had not told him how she was really feeling:

> I didn't realize it at the time, but I think she hadn't been all that well ... I thought a lot of her trouble was a recurrence [of polio] ... her problems were caused by that, but apparently, I think it was just plain old heart failure ... She probably did have the symptoms, but she wouldn't tell me.

The men believed that this pattern of not bothering them with symptoms of illness was one way women protected them. In a later section, I will discuss the explicit comments men made about what their wives did to protect them throughout their final illness.

Bob thought the doctor was treating his wife for fibromyalgia. In actuality, she had cancer that was 'working its way through the bone for three months, I'd say.' In the end, Bob's wife was diagnosed on a Monday and in a week and half, she was dead. Bob reiterated the level of shock, particularly because his wife 'was so healthy; she never went to a doctor.'

George, who did not fit the initial criteria for participation in the study, had been a widower for 23 years. He was 83 at the time of our interview and so had become a widower at 60. George's wife had died of Alzheimer's Disease, likely early-onset. George provided an extensive description of his wife's diagnosis. He started by explaining:

> She started doing some strange things, lapses of memory, a sense of deja-vu, a general disinterest in the world around her.

At first Katherine would not discuss the problem, but then one day asked to go for a drive, during which she told George that she thought she was going crazy. He and his sister-in-law took over the decision-making from then on. The initial diagnosis was restricted blood flow to the brain because Katherine's symptoms were atypical of Alzheimer's Disease. Surgery, however, disclosed 'classical symptoms of Alzheimer's.' George took care of Katherine at home until four years before her death when she needed so much care that she entered a nursing home. In his description, George used the 'causal argumentation and medical vocabulary' that are characteristic of 'extreme examples of the factual mode of speech' (Kirsi et al. 2000: 157). This approach allowed him to present the fragment of masculinity associated with a 'scientific attitude' (Rubin 2004).

For these widowers, the diagnosis was a singular moment in the story of their wives' illnesses, particularly a diagnosis of terminal illness. Once the men and their wives knew what was wrong, things simply progressed until the wives' deaths. At this point, some men adopted the mode of 'destiny speech' (Kirsi et al. 2000: 163). Now that there was nothing the widowers could do to affect the final outcome, they glossed over the details and appeared to be 'at the mercy of forces [i.e., the trajectories of terminal illness] beyond their control.' Several participants described this process as, 'downhill' from the point of diagnosis. The inevitability of the final outcome stands out as a crucial aspect of the story.

Angus, for example, explained that his wife had not been feeling well and had gone to the doctor on a Thursday. The doctor opined, 'Oh, you've got a touch, must be a touch of the flu. It's going around.' On Saturday, Mary said, 'I don't feel good at all; I'll go up to the Outpatients.' X-rays immediately showed a lump in her lung and then:

> Things just went downhill after that. We knew it was terminal right then, and she went right downhill and was in hospital.

Ed and Jacob both provided very detailed descriptions of their wives' symptoms using factual speech and switched to destiny speech when they got to the period after the diagnosis when everything was 'all downhill from there' or, as Marc put it, 'the end of it really,' even though she lived for two more years.

Several things stand out in these descriptions. First, several women hid, disguised, or downplayed the symptoms of illness that they were experiencing. This finding is particularly interesting, because it is usually men whom we think of as neglecting to go to a doctor when they experience symptoms of potentially serious illness (Smith et al. 2007). Second, a significant number of men reported either that the doctor originally thought their wives had a minor ailment, like the flu or an allergy, or that they felt that the doctor had minimized the seriousness of the situation. There were some cases in which the doctor reported high recovery rates, but the women were among the minority who had recurrences or did not respond to treatment. In two cases, the doctor either misdiagnosed the wife or was not entirely honest, while in at least one case the wife seems to have told her husband that her illness was less serious than she knew it was.

There were a few participants who stated briefly and simply what had caused their wives' deaths without any elaboration of the process of diagnosis. For example, Marcel stated that, 'she was sick for very close to three years – ovarian cancer.'

Along with the similarities in experience, there are characteristic ways that most participants talked about what had happened. I was immediately struck by the detail some of the men provided of the symptoms their wives experienced before diagnosis while they condensed the trajectories of their wives' illnesses after diagnosis. These recitations were generally spoken in a matter-of-fact manner, although a couple of the widowers did allow emotion to creep into their voices. This phenomenon may be an indication of men's inclination to deal with grief 'cognitively' by 'explaining the circumstances of their losses' rather than discussing their emotional reactions (Doka and Martin 2001: 43). As well, it may reflect their desire to understand what had happened through rehearsing and developing the story of their wives' deaths (Moore and Stratton 2002: 33).

There is also a striking amount of 'agency speech' in which the 'speaker adopts the identity of an independent actor' (Kirsi, Hervonen, and Jylhä 2000: 161) in the men's telling the story of their wives' deaths. Here the men and their contributions to the eventual diagnosis became the centre of the story. For example, when Winston's wife and her doctor both thought she had an allergy:

> After a time I didn't think so. And I had a conversation with [the doctor]. I told him why ... because of what I said, he sent her for some X-rays.

Winston recounts a similar process to explain what happened when his wife had severe headaches:

> I thought it was connected because they'd found a spot on her lungs ... I thought it had spread ... So I talked to the doctor about that. [emphasis added]

Although Winston was not able to control the outcome of his wife's cancer, he highlighted his role in encouraging the doctor to do the medical tests that were necessary.

Caregiving and Caring: It Had to Be Done

Agency speech is also noticeable in the way the men talked about the caring work they did while their wives were ill.[1] As others have reported (e.g., Calasanti and Bowen 2006; Davidson, Arber, and Ginn 2000), husbands are not at all hesitant to take up caregiving tasks when their wives require it. A number of the men characterised this taking care as simply work that had to be done (Stratton and Moore 2003). Some of these tasks reflected traditional male undertakings that communicated love for their wives. In describing these chores, the men used a combination of agency speech and the mode of 'familistic speech,' which highlighted their identities as husbands who were 'responsible caregiver[s]' (Kirsi et al. 2000: 157). For example, Leroy pointed out that he had fixed up the house for his wife:

> And then, oh my gosh, I had everything all fixed up for her before she died. I put in that new septic system back there. I bought that barn there behind me, bought that new oven ... did a lot of work in the kitchen here. New flash boards and everything on there. She was living then, of course.

Similarly, Ralph remarked:

> And she loved humming birds, and I had, I was never great – oh, I like flowers, but to me they were a bit of a pain because I had to plant them and weed them and everything else for her and for her alone. I had the walkway that you see there, and I had the window boxes and hanging flower pots ... I had pansies and all this stuff, and then I had other flowers for her.

For Herbert, whose wife had ALS, this work included acquiring, among other pieces of equipment, an appropriate electric wheelchair without paying the $12,000 it would have cost for a new one. He claimed some measure of expertise when he referred to himself, not without some pride, as a 'professional scrounger.'

It would be misleading, however, to imply that the men did not do any personal caring for their wives. Most participants did not elaborate on what they did, both preserving the dignity of their wives and avoiding identification with feminine tasks. However, the clues are there. Izzy, when describing how his life had changed since his wife died, for example, noted that he now had a:

> completely new way of life. To get away from the routine that you developed taking care of your wife. Because that couple of years, you've been doing that.

When I asked directly what kinds of things he had done, he declined to expand on those general comments.

In contrast, Matthew, whose wife had had a long-term progressive illness that he did not name, explained that:

> Toward the last six months, it was just like looking after a baby. She couldn't feed herself; she couldn't control her body functions ... it was

continual up and down all night and all day long, and she had dementia toward the end, and it wasn't fun.

Matthew noted that about two years before she 'finally' died, he had a breakdown. He explained that he was sent to a psychologist who suggested that the only solution was for him to leave his wife. He used a combination of familistic speech and the notion of reciprocity to explain why he rejected this advice. He commented:

> I said, 'maybe some men can, but I couldn't do that.' Because I know if I were ill, she wouldn't leave me ... I never went back, just got on doing what I had to do.

Matthew was one of two men – the other was George, whose wife had died of Alzheimer's disease – who said that after his wife's death, he felt like 'someone had lifted a thousand-pound weight off my shoulders.'

Some men emphasized that they took care of their wives alone. Their definition of the situation allowed them to project the masculine attributes of autonomy and self-reliance onto the situation even though they did receive help from others. Herbert, for example, explained that 'they' wanted to provide a homemaker to help him. He said that he could:

> get along alone. 'Oh no, you can't do it alone,' [they said]. And I said, 'Yes, I can do it alone.'

Herbert had two 'handicapped' children for whom he and his wife had cared for many years, and he was already familiar with the tasks involved in personal care. Second, and more interesting for the purposes of this chapter, is that he was not exactly alone. One daughter came down at night to bathe his wife while his other daughter:

> Every Thursday, would come down about 8:00 in the morning. And she told me, 'You get out of here. Don't come back until supper time.' And then [his wife's sister], she'd come down at noon and stay until I come back around supper time. So I had Tuesdays off ... and that was all the help we needed really.

As well, the Extramural Hospital nurses visited his home every day. Because he did not accept the additional care that had been offered, Herbert defined his rejection of the offer of a homemaker as 'doing it alone.'

It was not unusual for the men to receive help from their families. Bob, for example, had still been working when his wife was ill, but his sister-in-law stopped in or called every day to see if she needed anything. Angus also depended on family, in his case his daughter, to look after his wife while he was at work. In addition, he:

> had to get up, you know, at all hours and give her her pills ... would have to write down 'blue one at 3:00.'

As others have found (e.g., Rose and Bruce 1995: 14), the men talked about their taking care of their wives with a sense of accomplishment and appeared in the stories as 'rescuers and protectors.' Al, for example, believed that he had kept his wife alive longer by:

> making her eat and drink, watching her. I had a program for her medications, and I even drove her to visit her family. And I think I extended her life by attending to her.

Al wondered if he had done the right thing because his wife's inability to do things for herself affected her 'quality of life':

> Even though I was doing everything for her. She wasn't able to do it for herself. So I often wondered if I should have done that.

Some men's wives spent time in hospital or in a nursing home before they died. In those cases, they described frequent visits and carrying out tasks such as feeding their wives. Their comments reflect a sense of accomplishment reflected in the dedication and expertise they had as husbands. Winston, for one, went to the hospital for every meal:

> Because she might need some help or she might need something. Because by then I was feeding her.

Charles expressed, with pride, the opinion that his faithfulness in being at the hospital with his wife all day was probably unusual:

> And I don't know if many, I shouldn't generalize on this thing, but I was there from 7:00 in the morning until somewhere in the neighbourhood of 8:00 or 9:00 at night. Every single night she was in the hospital.

Perhaps the men's philosophy of taking care of their wives is best summed up by George who said:

> Looking back, I don't know how I did it. It didn't require any particular
> courage or any ability on my part. It was just simply a job that was there;
> it had to be done.[2]

This statement sums up a demanding situation in which a man just finds himself (destiny). Although he does not claim to have been particularly heroic, his approach is masculine: there was a job to be done, and I arose to the challenge; I just did it.

Description of Wives during their Illnesses:
And She Never Complained

In addition to describing what they did and how they felt, many of the participants talked about how their wives had handled being terminally ill. Most used this description as a chance to speak of their wives with admiration. As well, they talked about whether or not their wives or they took the opportunity to talk about the fact that the wives were dying and, for a few, the impact their wife's being a nurse had on her approach to her illness.

Fighting illness and never giving up are approaches that are currently admired and even linked to length of survival (Seale 1995, 2002), and several husbands did, indeed, admire their wives' fighting spirits. Herbert described his wife as stronger than he while Marc and Keith said that their wives did not give up 'until the end of her awareness, as long as she was awake' (Marc).

Leroy's wife lasted longer than the doctors had predicted because she wanted to experience one last Christmas:

> But she waited for Christmas. She wanted to see Christmas. So she did
> that. She was a fighter. Soon as Christmas was over, she went downhill,
> and three days later, she was dead.

Seven of the widowers explicitly praised their wives as being easy to care for or for not complaining about how they felt.[3] Herbert, for example, commented that his wife 'wasn't hard to care for. She wasn't a complainer.' Angus's wife was an exception. She remarked, 'It's awful hard to die.'

The men saw not complaining was a way their wives protected them, and three men explicitly identified other ways their wives protected them. Both Winston and Grant explained that their wives preferred being in the hospital because they felt that taking care of them was too much work for their husbands:

> [It was] her idea to go to the hospital. 'Cause she thought I was rushing around too much trying to help her, and that's what she said. [When she was in the hospital] she'd often say to me, 'Winston, why don't you sit down?' (Winston)

Some widowers said their wives protected them by not discussing their impending deaths. Keith characterized himself as a 'big baby' when it came to talking about his wife's dying. Therefore:

> I never said anything. Maybe that was why she didn't mention it. She never mentioned it again.

In response to my directly asking participants if they and their wives had talked about their dying or what their own lives would be like after the death, nine men said that they had talked while five said that they had not. These stories cover the full gamut of 'awareness contexts,' as developed by Glaser and Strauss (1965), from open awareness contexts through mutual pretense, suspicion to a closed context in which the husband kept the knowledge of the wife's impending death from her or she from him. In the open awareness context, everyone knows and agrees that the person is dying, while in mutual pretence, everyone knows the person is dying but pretends that she might recover. In the suspicion awareness context, one party believes that the ill person is going to die and imagines that others know, but will not admit, that this is the case. Finally, in the closed awareness context, no one discusses the possibility that an illness is terminal.

When there was an open awareness context, the couples talked about how the wives wanted their funeral to be handled. Several men, for example, said that their wives had expressed a desire to be cremated (or in one case not cremated) while one woman, Marcel's wife, had planned her own funeral.

Some women used the open awareness context to encourage their husbands to remarry:

She knew she was dying, and she, we even talked about that. And she more or less indicated that I should ... find another mate ... She was in agreement that I should need somebody. (Leroy)

Grant and his wife used the nine months during which they knew she was dying to talk as much as they could. This pleasure in conversation characterized Grant's marriage. He explained that he and his wife had never gotten a dishwasher because they enjoyed the companionship of doing the dishes together and talking. Grant provided a list of topics about which he and his wife had talked:

We talked for nine months ... about children ... our past life ... all the things we were thankful for. And the fact that she was facing death ... we got rid of everything we needed to get rid of ... some forgiving ... on both sides ... mostly happy talk.

Several widowers, in contrast, experienced what Glaser and Strauss (1965) referred to as mutual pretence, a situation in which both they and their wives pretended that they were unaware that she was dying. For example:

No, we didn't talk about death at all, you know. I knew she was dying, and I think she knew it, too. We more or less stayed off the subject ... as if she were going to get better. But I knew she wouldn't get better. (Tim)

Other instances resemble the suspicion awareness context (Glaser and Strauss 1965), in which the individuals involved suspect that the ill person is dying, but neither addresses the issue directly. In these cases, either the wife or the husband seemed to have protected the other although even here it is uncertain whether both knew what was going on. Keith, for example, believed that his wife knew she was dying because she was a nurse:

She must have known what was going on. But she never let on to any of us or never said anything to any of us. (Keith)

Bernie conformed to a closed-awareness context by keeping his wife's terminal diagnosis from her:

I have been living with my wife's death ... the doctor told me ... it was a matter of time. He never let her know, or she was still optimistic. And I nursed that optimism along. I didn't want her to ever stop being optimistic. (Bernie)

Bob and his wife both knew she was dying, but he did not know how to bring up the subject. As the following quote indicates, Bob would have liked to have gotten the answers to some very practical questions:

> She knew [she was dying]. [Did you talk about it?] No, we didn't. There was a lot of things I would have liked to have asked, but how do you ask something when you know they're going to die? It would have been hard for her ... She didn't answer some of them things. Like I knew where she wanted to be buried. But other than that, I didn't. I had to do everything on my own because she didn't tell me.

There was a plaintiveness in the tone of Bob's comments that lead one to believe that his wife let him down by not taking care of things that were normally her responsibility.

Three participants explained that their wives seemed to have talked to their children rather than to them about what was happening. They seemed frustrated or even hurt that their wives had not confided in them. Chad, for example, said that his wife:

> never acknowledged the fact that she was dying. She denied she was bad. I didn't know.

His wife had left instructions about her funeral with his son. He said: 'So this is what makes me doubt that she had any idea.'

An additional element of the wives' approach to dying for four of the widowers was the fact of their being nurses. All four commented that their wives must have known what was going on and what was going to happen because of their medical experience:

> Joyce was a nurse, a registered nurse. So she knew pretty well what stage she was at. (Grant)

Others described suspicion awareness context using phrases such as 'she must have known' (Keith). For Chad, his wife's being a nurse only increased his suspicion that she knew she was dying but did not share that knowledge with him. Again, his words portray a sense of betrayal, a characteristic of suspicion awareness context:

But she was a nurse ... But did she tell me all she knew? ... There's a lot of things that happened since she passed away that give me doubts ... a little handwritten will with all her personal items.

For some of these men, their wives' being nurses raised the possibility that they had been involved in a closed awareness context. Their wives probably knew they were dying but did not share the information with their husbands.

The Inevitable

Most of the participants were astonishingly brief in their description of what happened when their wives actually died. Four made very terse comments, for example, 'a hard, hard death' (Tim) and 'That was it' (Izzy). George and Matthew, whose wives had had long-term, progressive illnesses, never directly talked about their wives' deaths. Others focused on particular aspects of what happened when their wives died. Themes include the decision to stop therapeutic treatment or not to use heroic measures,[4] surprise at when or how quickly she died, her being unconscious at the end, his knowing or being able to interpret her wishes, being with her at the moment of death, and the time of her death being in God's hands.

The notion of the 'good death' appeared in the stories of five men who pointed out that they and/or their wives had decided that they did not want her life extended through technology (Auger 2000: 68). This decision was a way of controlling at least some aspects of the dying process. Herbert, whose wife had had ALS, explained that she did not want to be put on a ventilator because 'she didn't want to be here if she couldn't communicate' while Ralph, whose wife had Alzheimer's Disease, told the doctors, whatever is going to take place, 'let it take place.' Three of the Florida widowers talked about heroic measures and living wills. Charles, for example, in explaining the type of hospital his wife was in said:

Not a hospice in the true sense of the word. It's a hospital, but they don't take any heroic measures.

Samuel only came to understand how close his wife was to death when the staff at Sloan Kettering told him and his wife:

We won't use any heroic measures. And of course, that scared us ... She had signed the form that they wouldn't use heroic measures to keep her alive.

For some, death was sudden or came faster than expected. Stephen and his wife were living in an assisted-living facility when 'she was in the bathroom and fell down, and that was it' while Stan's wife died of sudden heart failure. Patrick expressed the suddenness of his wife's death this way:

> She was diagnosed on a Monday, and a week and a half later, she was dead.

The starkness of his language communicates well the depth of his shock and how quickly his wife succumbed to cancer after the diagnosis.

Three wives were sufficiently drugged at the end that they were either unable to communicate or were unconscious. Being drugged may have accelerated their deaths. Angus described the effect of a new medication:

> That night she slept ... but she was awful groggy the next day ... but she was awake. But that night and then next day, she seemed to go down ... very sleepy ... then about 9:00 that night, she got right up out of bed, sat right up and said, 'I can't breathe. I can't breathe,' then collapsed.

Chad regretted that he had not been warned that 'shooting Ativan and morphine' would render his wife unconscious. He felt that he had missed out on something important as a result of his wife's being drugged at the end of her illness.

In stark contrast are the widowers who talked about their being the people who knew what their wives wanted or who understood their situation when others did not. Here, agency speech once again emerges. Herbert, for example, commented that he had to listen closely, but 'I could tell what she wanted done and how she wanted everything.'

Other men invoked a form of destiny speech. Ralph explained that he told the doctors not to be sorry that his wife had died because:

> It's God's blessing because she never wanted to go into a nursing home ... so it all ended up with God in His own way, looked after everything because she got everything she wanted.

Being with their wives at the time of their death allowed the men to fulfill their obligations as husbands. Five participants explicitly pointed out that they were with their wives when they died. Al underlined the importance through repetition:

I was there when she did pass away. I stayed with her nights. And I was there when she passed away. Right, right, I was right with her.

Charles used repetition to underline the importance of not only his but also his children's being there when his wife died, even though she had been in a semi-coma for a couple of weeks:

But my son was there, my daughter was there, and my daughter-in-law was there. We were all there when she passed away.

Two men indicated that it was the doctor rather than they who had the authority to decide that their wives had passed away. Because of this definition of the situation, that is, a person is not dead until a doctor says so, the men did not react to their wives' deaths until the doctor confirmed the situation. Grant, for example, was with his wife when the pulse in her neck stopped, but:

Of course, I'm not a doctor. I couldn't say she's dead. So I called for a nurse. She said, 'Yes, I get no heartbeat, no pulse.' Then the doctor ... did his examination.

Only after the doctor had been there, had Joyce officially died. Similarly, Bernie did not react to his wife's death until the doctor 'made the pronouncement; [then] I broke down.'

Two characteristics of the widowers' narrations about the diagnosis and the physical progression of their wives' dying stand out. First, the men discussed these issues in great detail which, in the description of symptoms, were often explicit. Nonetheless, the trajectory of their wives' illnesses after the terminal diagnosis was barely mentioned, and the participants simply commented that 'it was all downhill' from then until death. This reflects a period during which they had no control over what happened except in the area of doing things for and taking care of their wives.

Second, is the employment of 'agency speech' in various widowers' discussions of their role in encouraging doctors to do further tests and the things they did for their wives. The men appear as central actors who played an active part in the diagnosis of their wives' illnesses. The women also come more alive in the recounting of their deaths than in any other part of the interviews. Familistic descriptions allow them to appear as loving wives who protected their husbands from overwork, who never complained, and who fought to the very end. Thus, in what might seem a situation in which both spouses were almost powerless, we see the development of a 'heroic narrative' (Doucet 2007: 62-3) in which the husband did what he had to do, and the wife conformed to contemporary norms of fighting death until the end with a cheerful countenance (Seale 2002).

In Chapter Four, we shall see a similar style in the men's discussion of what happened next. It captures the variety of immediate reactions the widowers reported as well as their decisions about funerals and the sorting out of the necessary paperwork. The men had crossed the border into a foreign country and had to begin the long process of adapting to their new situation.

4 Early Days of Widowhood

The immediate aftermath of the death of their wives brought the widowers into a new stage of their lives, one that many were not ready to face. Some participants were quite reserved about their feelings while others, most notably the Florida group, expressed strong emotional reactions. Many discussed the support they had gotten from their family, friends, and fellow church members. Comments about how their wives' funerals were planned were quite diverse. Many men's strongest memory of the funeral is the large number of people who attended, which they felt communicated the respect and fondness many friends and colleagues felt for their wives.

During this period, the men also had to complete much necessary paperwork, and the following pages discuss how they described this task and what it meant to them. For many, the paperwork was nothing out of the ordinary, but some described having to show their wives' death certificates over and over as well as frustration with bureaucratic or incompetent staff at government offices.

Immediate Reactions: You're in a State of Shock

Although the interviews were, in general, notable for the participants' reserve, it was in their discussion of what they remembered about the time right after their wives died that some men talked about their emotions. Six of the men did not refer at all to emotions in their discussions of their wives' deaths including Ralph, who referred to his wife as 'my darling' throughout the interview. Elizabeth Levang (1998) suggests that men do not have a language or vocabulary for grief; most of these men confirmed this, but the two social contexts led to very different vocabularies of emotion.

The Florida interviews were distinctive for the level of expressiveness in the descriptions of the early days of widowhood and in the richness of their vocabulary of emotions. This group referred to 'breaking down completely' (Ed), 'being despondent' (Al), 'experiencing the first month as a nightmare' (Samuel), experiencing a 'very, very sad time' (Charles), and:

> You really don't know what to do or who you are ... panic-stricken ... just trying to find out who the hell you are and what you are doing. (Bernie)

Izzy's interview was relatively short, and he showed some impatience at my probing questions. However, it was Izzy, whose wife had died eight years earlier, who was the most eloquent in his description of how terrible he felt right after his wife's death:

> At the beginning ... very, very difficult ... tremendous shock ... completely out of it ... feel like giving up ... all of a sudden, you're completely on your own, completely alone ... a big blow ... of course, you're miserable, and you miss her so much, and the surroundings remind you of her ... mad that I didn't have enough years, angry ... very angry and upset ... At the beginning I was very lonesome ... There was a vacancy, a huge void ... I felt very angry because she was too young.

The most common words the men used to describe their emotional state right after their wives died were 'shock,' 'numbness,' 'in a daze.' In contrast, Mel, whose wife had been ill for many years, commented that he had done his grieving 'for years beforehand. So it didn't come as a shock.' Even men whose wives had been ill a long time sometimes talked about being shocked or feeling numb.

Five men said that they cried either immediately after their wives died, for example, Grant who 'sobbed like a baby,' 'or later on.' Chad explained that crying 'helped to relieve the pressure' and that he had been told by his:

> lady minister to 'go ahead and cry if you feel like it.' And I did, I didn't make no bones about it.

In contrast, Stan, identifying himself with the stoicism of masculinity, with some disapproval said that:

> Some people go around moaning and crying. I can't do that. It's just one of those things. I just try to keep busy.

Anxiety and general psychological distress are not uncommon among widowers, and the participants' comments reflect this phenomenon along with an unwillingness to describe themselves as depressed (Steeves & Kahn 2005). Leroy, for example, takes 'happy pills' prescribed by his doctor. Although he was 'doing fine' at the beginning, as time went on, he 'was getting pretty down in the mouth.' A few men mentioned that they had slipped into the practice of drinking alcohol regularly after their wives died. All, like Conrad, asserted that when they realized that they were becoming dependent, they stopped drinking. Conrad replaced his alcohol consumption with trips to the gym to work out. Notably, the three men exhibited self control by finding ways to master their drinking without seeking professional help.

A small group of men were troubled at first by strong negative images. Keith noted that his wife had looked practically like a skeleton at the end, and he compared her appearance to photos of Holocaust survivors. Grant found himself dwelling on:

> This horrible picture of her lying in that cold grave. And Lord knows what's getting in that coffin with her. Not very pleasant thoughts.

Three of the men made a point of explaining that one simply has to accept what has happened. Chad couched his opinion in religious terms:

> I mean, we all believe we're going to heaven ... it helps you to accept that you can't change what's already happened.

A more secular approach was simple fatalism or simply accepting the situation as 'just one of those things '(Stan).

Finally, although men who had cared for their wives for a long time took pride in managing to care for them in the face of almost overwhelming difficulty, they admitted that they felt relief when their wives died. George, whose wife had had Alzheimer's Disease, was relieved that his wife's 'ordeal was over' while Matthew, whose wife had had a long-term, progressively debilitating disease, felt that a huge weight had been lifted from his shoulders.

It is in the days immediately following a death that widowers can expect family, friends, and neighbours to surround them. This feeling of support helps them to get through the first difficult days of grieving.

The next section discusses what the widowers said about the attention they received.

Support: An Invasion of Food and Attention

A number of the participants described the support they had received from fellow congregation members, friends and family even in light of the decrease in ritual surrounding a death (Gorer 1965). They were moved by the support and sometimes interpreted it as an indication of the affection people had for their wives.

Congregation members did not disappoint widowers who were very active in their churches. Herbert and Mel talked about receiving food and visits. Patrick commented that he did not need many visits from his fellow parishioners because he was often at the church. He described the support he got from the church members as:

friendship, prayer support and friendship support, moral support.

Others talked about friends and neighbours. Leroy's friends gave 'help, food, caring,' while Marcel described experiencing 'an invasion of food and attention.' Several widowers expressed surprise at how much people cared. Whereas in Canada people brought food, in Florida, where socializing often takes place in restaurants, friends and neighbours showed their support by thinking to call and make sure the widowers went out to dinner with various people.

A few men focused on the support of family. Patrick said that his family was his 'mainstay,' while Herbert's daughter came from another province and stayed two weeks. Leonard and Stan both commented on the support and help they received from their wives' families. Three men described trips they took either with family or to visit family soon after their wives' deaths as helping them to get through that period.

Two activities characterize the early days of widowhood: planning and participating in a funeral and completing necessary paperwork. The next few pages will look at what the widowers said about these two elements.

The Funeral

Most of the participants talked at some length about their wives' funerals. Topics they discussed included to what extent they followed their wives' wishes, how the funeral was planned, the nature of family involvement, and what the actual funeral was like. The (Jewish) Florida sample seemed to have wrestled with fewer decisions or dilemmas about planning the funeral, perhaps because the rituals of sitting *shiva*[1] and having an immediate funeral are still fairly standard for Jews (Stratton & Moore 2003).

Several widowers described the funeral as something that they had had to get 'over with' (Herbert) or the planning of which they 'dreaded' (Leonard). Samuel was most explicit in his dislike of the Jewish mourning rituals, which he characterized as 'a nightmare' and remarked, 'Thank God it was over.' For the Canadian men who had to wait for the ground to thaw before their wives could be buried (Leroy and Stan), the wait was a long one. Leroy, in particular, explained that the wait for his wife's burial delayed 'closure.'

Several widowers commented that they followed their wives' wishes about the nature of their funeral and/or where and what they wanted to have done with their remains. At one end of the spectrum, Marcel's wife planned everything. The importance of her having done the planning is evident through Marcel's repetition of the phrase, 'she planned':

> She planned the funeral. She planned to be cremated, and she planned who was to sing in the church. Everything.

At the other end of the spectrum, we find Chad, whose wife:

> didn't want any funeral or anything. She wanted to be cremated ... No visitation. No nothing.

Chad did not follow his wife's wishes. He believed that everyone should have a funeral. His wife, therefore, would have one, too. He introduced two rationales for his going ahead with a funeral against his wife's wishes:

> I know from experience that if people don't get to talk to you at the time, the next time they see you coming down the sidewalk, they'll cross the street rather than meet you ... [and] I did believe that if you die, you should have a funeral. Period ... Like the minister said, funerals are for the living more than the dead, maybe ... It just makes you feel good to have a nice funeral.

Just as Chad had invoked the authority of his minister to legitimate his crying when his wife died, he also used her authority to justify his decision to have a funeral. Chad's wife had wanted:

to go the cheap way. Apparently, you can be cremated just in ... these cardboard boxes ... she didn't want to be embalmed ... She just wanted to go au naturel.

Chad did comply with this request and spread her ashes as she had asked.

Although some men pleased themselves in their decisions about the funeral, they were unanimous in following their wives' wishes about burial and/or cremation. A number of the women wanted to be cremated, and the men carried out their requests (Samuel, Leonard, Ralph, Chad). As well, a few of the widowers commented that their wives had wanted to be buried in a particular place, for example in her family plot (Stan) or 'up on a hill overlooking the river' (Ralph). They took pride, as husbands, in the fulfilment of those desires.

Leonard initially abided by his wife's desire not to have a funeral, but:

As time went on, it became more and more important for me to have something like a funeral ... What we did then was to have a memorial service when we planted the flowers and planted the ashes underneath. And that was really a funeral.

In this way, he felt that he went along with his wife's wishes and also satisfied his need to have a ceremony in her honour.

Ralph took pride in explaining that his wife had gotten everything she wanted. His providing exactly what she had asked for was an expression of his love for her:

She didn't want to go into a nursing home, she wanted to be cremated, she wanted a lunch for everybody after the service, she got that, and she was buried where she wanted ... So she's buried where she wanted to be, and I had done the best I could.

All of these arrangements took planning, and there was great diversity in the way the men talked about how their wives' funerals got planned. Only two widowers remarked that they had had little to nothing to do with making the arrangements: Marcel, whose wife planned everything, and Stephen who explained:

I don't really know. It just happened. I didn't plan the thing, no ... My son came ... took over more or less ... He was responsible and took over the whole thing. He's a well organized person. And I had nothing to do

with it, and I never bothered to think about it. I don't want to think
about it.

Stephen's attitude may reflect the fact that he was in the medical profession, where he could simply show up and find arrangements made as well as a traditional gender orientation in which the man simply expects to be taken care of.[2] In addition, the suddenness of his wife's death may have contributed to Stephen's abdicating the responsibility for the planning of her funeral. Finally, Stephen's advanced age – he was the only participant who was over 90 at the time of the interview – may have had an impact.

Adult children were often involved in planning funerals. Some men, for example, Angus, were clearly in charge and deliberately invited their children's participation:

But I had the kids all involved ... what they would like to do for their mother's funeral ... so they would feel a part of it. I didn't want to go and say ... we're going to do it this way. It was their mother, and I feel [they] should have a say ... So that's what we did.

In fact, Angus' entire description of planning his wife's funeral exhibited a sense of control and competence:

I did it ahead of time ... I've had several funerals to look after so I had a lot of experience ... If you go to the funeral parlours, you have to make the arrangements ... you've got to pick out the coffin, you've got to think of what they're going to wear, and who is going to be pall bearers, and ... where they're going to be buried and what arrangements you are going to make.

Angus' list of the plethora of tasks underlines his mastery and competence as a man over his lifetime. His children had a say because as a good father and husband, Angus made sure they were involved.

In other cases, the locus of control was more complicated. The heightened emotional atmosphere that follows a death led to stronger reactions than one might have in more ordinary times. Several women had communicated their wishes to their children while in other situations, there was simply a lack of agreement about certain aspects of the funeral. Keith commented that his daughters had wanted only the immediate family to attend and the casket closed. He noted that these issues can cause 'a few rifts in the family.' In the strong emotional climate of the moment, 'little things that really aren't important ... get to you at that time.'

Matthew seemed to be at odds, not only with his daughter, but with other members of the family who, he felt, had not paid enough attention to his wife when she was alive. His comments about what he would like when he dies make the hypocrisy he believes he observed at his wife's funeral explicit:

> No service, no nothing. Nobody standing around making silly promises – we're going to get together. And it's too bad we have to get together at funerals, and they don't mean it. You're never going to see them again, so the heck with it!

Most widowers, who talked about their children or wife's family in the context of the funeral, had only positive things to say. Children returned from out of town and accompanied their fathers to funeral homes while other members of her family may have helped with decision making. Leonard's in-laws affirmed his decision not to have a funeral right after his wife died, stayed a few days longer than they had planned when he asked, and helped him decide what to do with his wife's ashes.

Regardless of how the funeral got planned, for many men, the number of people who attended seemed to be its most significant characteristic.[3] Large attendance indicated the affection and respect people had for their wives. The men used repetition and superlatives to underline the significance of large crowds at the funeral:

> And the funeral was a big funeral. I mean there was no room left in the church ... a fair size church ... all the seats were taken. There was nothing, no room left. (Winston)

> It was the largest gathering of people ... her funeral was the largest that had ever been held. (George)

One Florida widower explained that the large number of people who attended his wife's funeral 'up north' (i.e., in New York City) was unusual for those who had retired to the Sunbelt. He invoked his rabbi to lend credence to his observation:

The Rabbi even mentioned the fact that he has the same type of funeral where people have been in Florida for 10, 15 years and come back ... because their plot is here, and there's a dozen people in the chapel. So, anyway, it was a good show. (Charles)

Ed had his wife's funeral 'up north,' but agreed to a friend's request to have a memorial for his wife in their condo's clubhouse. He may have been feeling a little sheepish when he remarked:

I mean, I'm not boasting, but the clubhouse was mobbed – from pillar to post.

Of course, Ed was boasting, but he was communicating his pride at the fondness for his wife that the crowded memorial made evident.

The size of the crowd indicated, for the widowers, the degree of affection (Winston) and respect (Charles, Grant) that neighbours, friends, and colleagues felt for their wives:

She was quite well known and born in this town ... and almost everybody in the village showed up. And then all her co-workers ... came as well. Comforting to know so many people respected her in that way. (Grant)

Leroy and Mel also talked about the upbeat nature of their wives' funerals. Leroy had had to wait months for his wife's burial, but when it did take place, people came from far and near:

We had that catered ... she had that table right full of lobsters ... We had a really big feed ... And we had a nice little party for her and all the gang ... It was a nice day, too ... a lot of reminiscing and quite light hearted, too ... not one of those teary things ... I think that's the way she would have wanted it.

Leroy is fairly secular, but Mel attributed the upbeat nature of his wife's funeral to his being Christian:

Sunday morning was a real, snappy little number [that my wife liked] ... So a lot of people that wouldn't have a lot of faith, they probably thought it was very odd, this happy piece to be sung at a funeral ... [a Catholic friend said], 'very odd funeral.'

There is an undertone of competition to the men's accounts of the size and atmosphere of the funerals. Reporting on very large, successful funerals puts them in a dominant position in the subordinate field of masculinity (Coles 2008) inhabited by old widowers.

For most men, the period of time right after the funeral was taken up with the paperwork involved with getting their affairs in order and changing things like bank accounts and the Canada Pension Plan. The next section looks at what they said about this process.

Paperwork

The participants had a variety of reactions to my asking if there had been a lot of paperwork to deal with in the aftermath of their wives' deaths. More men felt that the paperwork had not been a major issue for them than those who described the work as a lot or difficult. In addition, some men focused on the frustrations of bureaucracy and the requirement for them to show their wives' death certificates rather than on the intrinsic complexity of accomplishing the paperwork itself. A few talked about advice they had gotten from others while three spoke at length about getting what they were entitled to.

Seven participants stated that the paperwork had not been particularly onerous. Keith, for example, replied to my question about whether there had been a lot of paperwork by saying:

> No, she had her will made up. And I didn't think there was too much ... A lot of thank-you notes and stuff like that. But it's the norm, I guess.

It is striking that this group of widowers did not connect the filling out of forms for the Canada Pension Plan, banks, car registration or insurance, and other notifications with my asking about paperwork. The participants took these traditional male chores so for granted that they did not see the need to mention them or did not think of them as anything special. In fact, Charles was grateful about having had this busy work to do at that emotionally trying time.

Some men did, however, describe the paperwork as onerous. Mel felt that the work was straightforward, but:

> I was the executor. But we did have a will. And ... it was up to date. And so it was just a case of going to the lawyer that had done it and also the accountant ... a lot of loose ends. I mean, not only did I have to do that, but the things like advising Canada Pension and all that stuff. To me, it was quite complicated.

Leonard used a systematic strategy to get things figured out. He used a problem-solving approach that he might have borrowed from the workplace as Phyllis Braudy Harris (2005:222) suggests many men do when they act as caregivers:

> Well, I remember taking a week off just to go through all the financial stuff. And trying to figure out where we were. Cause she had handled the money ... I didn't have any idea where things were. So I got a computer program, Quicken ... I just took a week and went through. Called everybody from the phone company and figured out what our bills were and what our payments were ... It probably didn't require that long a time, but then it seemed like a humongous task.

But for most of the men who found the paperwork difficult, it was the bureaucracy or incompetence of agencies that made the paperwork frustrating rather than their own inexperience. George's comments are typical of the four widowers who complained:

> Oh, the government near drove me crazy. They wanted, they threatened to seize bank accounts and just do this and that. But there was all this paperwork for getting – she was on medical disability and I was entitled to a widowers' benefit and lots of paperwork.

For some, the need to provide a death certificate over and over was a problem. Herbert emphasized the unpleasantness of this requirement through repetition:

> I picked up the death certificate from the funeral home ... a bunch of paperwork, insurance claims ... And of course, they have to have a death certificate ... She had a [credit] card that she had insurance on, and they had to have a death certificate.

Marc noted that he had needed eight copies of the death certificate to comply with all the bureaucratic requirements. Having to show a death certificate is one of the more emotionally difficult aspects of early widowhood for both men and women (van den Hoonaard 2001).

One striking phenomenon was three widowers' sense of pride at getting money that was due to them. Two, in particular, went on at length to illustrate this accomplishment. Chad, for example, was very persistent in his efforts to get customer loyalty points from two different stores:

If you follow all these money grabbers' wishers. Like I went to [the store];
I knew she used to have [their] credit card. And she had [their customer-
loyalty card]. So I went in one day, probably two months after to try and
to transfer her ... points to my name. No way in hell. No, they wanted a
copy of her will ... They wanted her death certificate ... So that kind of
ticked me off. I was getting kind of ugly at that point. It was stupid ... They
say, 'Well, maybe you kicked her out and you're trying to take all her
stuff.' And all this stuff. And I said, 'Well, does she owe you any money?'
They wouldn't tell me that either. So finally, I said to the girl, 'Well, I hope
she does ... You're going to have to find her to get it.' And I never heard
from them after that.

Chad is still fighting with a second store to get the points he feels he is
entitled to. Similarly, Herbert reported having 'months and months and
months' when he 'called and sent letters' before getting the life insurance benefit from a major credit card company. These widowers were
fighting for what they saw as legally coming to them and were willing
to expend a great deal of energy to win the fight. Their stories have a
theme of 'winning' that is familiar in men's stories which portray them
as 'lone heroes pitted against the odds' (Coates 2003:196).

In contrast, others pointed out to George and Marc what they were
entitled to. George discovered that he had been shortchanged by the
government three years after his wife's death. He gave credit to 'little
Amy' for his success. She had told him:

'My goodness, they owe you a lot of money. I'll try to get it back for you
... I don't know if I can; it's never been done.' But she did.

Marc found out what he was entitled to from 'the gal' at the union.
These payments included life insurance on a car loan, a union life-
insurance policy and death benefits from the Canada Pension Plan.
Marc also benefited from the kindness and competence of officials like
the bank officer who reminded him about the life-insurance policy on
his car loan.

Three other widowers depended on advice to complete the proper
paperwork. Bob depended on the occupational association to which his
wife had belonged to get him started, and:

I just went from there ... got started. And I had to get her cancelled off.
And then you had her [occupational] pension. And like I had to go to the

bank and get things straightened out there ... And just kept working from there.

Winston, reflecting a more middle-class approach, depended on his lawyer.

One might expect that, with the widespread use of computerized record keeping, there would be less paperwork and less obligation to continually have to produce copies of a loved one's death certificate. There seems to have been no progress in minimizing this bureaucratic work. The participants listed off many paperwork chores that impress one both with their onerousness and with the competence the men displayed in their descriptions.

Although *By Himself* is not about grief or grieving per se, in talking about the early days of widowhood, the men did bring up aspects of grieving. In the fairly new and small amount of research that talks about how men grieve, there is almost no discussion about widowers. For example, Elizabeth Levang's book, *When Men Grieve: Why Men Grieve Differently & How You Can Help* (1998), uses vignettes of a variety of circumstances which might bring about grieving. This book talks about loss of children, being left by a wife, and loss of parents, jobs, and physical ability. It does not provide a single example of a widower's experience.

Scott Campbell and Phyllis Silverman's book, *Widower: When Men Are Left Alone* (1996), reinforces the participants' comments about feeling shock and numbness in the early days of widowhood. They have also noted that many men do not have the vocabulary to express their feelings and their grief. This lack of vocabulary is evident in the stories of some Canadian widowers.

It is in this area of the interviews that men were most likely to show emotion. Agency speech, a claim of mastery, and invoking others' approval of crying or otherwise betraying emotion may serve to counterbalance the potential challenge to these participants' sense of themselves as men presented by this situation in which they were both powerless and suffered a great loss.

The men used keeping busy and completing paperwork as strategies to cope with the strong emotions of the early days of widowhood. These activities also have helped the men to 'avoid feelings of loneliness or self pity' and facilitated their keeping 'positive' (Crummy 2002: 60). They worked as a 'line of defence' against grief that otherwise might have overwhelmed these widowers (Steeves and Kahn 2005: 201).

The men looked to areas of their own mastery on which to focus when telling these emotion-laden stories. The men who exerted a great deal of effort in order to obtain store loyalty points and other small financial entitlements used these activities to reinforce a sense of purpose and self-reliance in their lives as well as their commitment to right and wrong (Lund and Caserta 2001: 165). Overcoming frustrating challenges provides an example of the widowers' accomplishments that add another 'fragment' to their claims of masculinity. The amount of money involved was often negligible; it was winning the battle and being right that counted.

After the very early days of being a widower had passed, the men had to find ways to negotiate their relationships with their adult children, with friends, and with women. The next few chapters address these issues.

PART THREE

Negotiating Relationships with Others

5 Widowers' Relationships with Their Children

Many authors have suggested that, because women are the traditional kinkeepers, widowers might find that their relationships with their children deteriorate or become more distant when their wives are no longer around to mediate and arrange visits. Although this phenomenon is undoubtedly true for some men, the widowers' descriptions of these relationships were more complex and diverse than this generalization might suggest.

As Alinde Moore and Dorothy Stratton discovered in *Resilient Widowers*, adult children play a variety of roles in their widowed fathers' lives. They note that these children:

> provided emotional support ... participated in social activities with their fathers ... provided specific help with [housework] ... were a local or long-distance telephone contact ... gave care when it was needed, and ... received things from their fathers, such as advice, money, and companionship. (2002: 178)

The men to whom I spoke also described a wide variety of ways that their children[1] participated in their lives. However, it is not only the specific things that children did, but the way the fathers talked about their relationship with those children, that will be the focus of this chapter. The first section looks at how the men talked about their children in general, followed by a discussion of the fathers' perceptions regarding how intrusive their children, particularly their daughters, were following their mothers' death.

Many of the adult children have taken over family occasions that had previously been the purview of their parents, for example, the hosting of holiday meals, and it is to this phenomenon that the chapter turns next. The fathers still retained their role as father, and this is evident in the way they discussed their children's problems and what they were doing or had done to assist their children.

Finally, the chapter will discuss the widowers' observations about their children's relationships with their mothers as well as the specific ways their daughters interacted with them because of their gendered role as women. In conclusion, part of the fathers' reactions to their relationships with their children, especially daughters, reflects a sense of ambivalence.

General Comments about Relationships:
They Have Their Own Families

Although these widowers had varied relationships with their children, most of them seemed to be satisfied with the ones they described. They talked about regular visiting and phone calls, increased levels of communication, and closer relationships in the time since their wives' deaths. Nonetheless, there were men who described unhappy or distant relationships. Several men had at least one child with whom they had irregular or no contact, although all the men were in close touch with at least one adult child. A few men had children who were living with them when their wives died, two of whom still had an adult child living at home at the time of the interview. One widower had shared an apartment with his son for a short while after his wife's death. None of the men had moved in with a child.

The geographic location of the widowers also had an impact on their relationships with their children. The Florida widowers' children still lived 'up north,' thus allowing for 'intimacy at a distance' (Rosenmayr 1977). These relationships had more latitude, and both the fathers and the adult children participated less directly in each other's lives. In contrast, the Canadian widowers generally had at least one child who lived relatively nearby. This allowed for more day-to-day reciprocity, but it also provided the possibility for more conflict, particularly if a daughter were critical of the way her father was living his life.

Both implicit and explicit in the way the participants talked about their connections with their adult children was the normative recognition that those children had responsibilities to their own families that might result in less contact than the fathers might have wanted. Those fathers would argue that the priority their children give 'to their own families' is appropriate and 'the way it should be.' Grant, for example, noted that his children invited him for lunches and family functions. But:

> They have their own families, and they're wrapped up in them, of course.
> Sometimes a few days go by before they check on me ... [They're] busy
> with their own families and don't think about calling Dad until perhaps 9
> or 10 o'clock at night. And that's the way it should be. They should look
> after their families first.

Children rallied around their fathers right after their mothers had
died, and some men were taken aback when they reverted to their
usual relationship. Marc, for example, replied to my question about
anything that had surprised him by saying:

> It's the abruptness with which the expression of sympathy surrounds you
> at the time and then equally the abruptness with which it is all gone. Your
> relatives are gone, your children are gone. They return to their duties and
> functions as parents and as working people, and then you're left to your
> own resources. And then you have to cope.

Similarly, Izzy pointed out that his relationship with his children had
become closer right after his wife's death but has since reverted to
the way it had been when she was alive. Similar to widows, the men
accepted the fact that their children were quite busy with jobs and
families and often used this busyness to justify seeing their children
less than they would have liked. For the most part, the men expected
their children to take primary responsibility for calling and initiating
visits. This kinkeeping role had fallen to their wives when they were
alive, and the men were reluctant to take it up. They seemed unaware
that they might have seen their children more often if they had taken
the initiative.

The widowers in Florida faced a different situation because most of
their children lived 'up north.' When the grandchildren had been
young, they and their parents had visited more often, but once the
grandchildren got a little older, the visits generally became more infre-
quent. It, thus, fell to the widowers to go up north to visit their children.
They kept those visits short because their children and grandchildren
were busy at work and school:

> Next time [I visit] it will be just for long weekends ... That's enough. They
> both work; their kids are off in school. What am I going to do alone all
> day? Which is silly. You watch the dog. (Ed)

Nonetheless, when I asked the participants whether their relationship with their children had changed in any way since their wive's deaths, there were several who commented that the relationship had become closer. Grant, for example, found that his children had begun to verbalize their feelings more:

> I think that I'm a little closer to my children ... Although ... I [always] told [the boys] that I loved them ... they have started now to say that to me ... My daughter always did, but the boys have changed somewhat.

Others, using a light tone, communicated their children's realization that they might not live forever. Mel, for example, remarked dryly that his daughter, 'calls me every day to see if I'm still alive.'

Marc noted that not only had his children become closer to him, but he also found himself more interested in his children's lives:

> I would say we became closer, and I noticed that I became ... much more interested in their ... comings and goings and their successes and their plans; the vicissitudes if there were any ... This type of thing. Yeah, there was a closer bond, no question to that.

This mutual concern with each other's lives characterizes how Marc's relationship with his children has changed. There is more fun and enjoyment for Marc in this change.

Marcel explained that his relationship with his children had been more patriarchal when his wife was alive. The transition to widowhood changed his way of being a father. He explained:

> Perhaps I am more tolerant now ... Before I was more in the role of an Italian father, and now I am just like a normal human being with [other] human beings who have to make their own decisions. Before I was a little bit tough on them ... We are closer now.

Similar to Marcel, other widowers acknowledged that their children had to make their own decisions, and they, therefore, actively refrained from trying to influence their children more than they or the children thought was appropriate. These men, recognizing 'unspoken boundaries around communication' (Peters et al. 2006: 548), avoided personal conversations with their children and described placid but distant relationships. Edward, for example, commented that, although his son lives with him, and he talks to his daughter every week:

I don't push them, you know ... or being too nosy ... I might, if they asked something, I give them my opinion and let it go at that ... but I don't get involved, you know, [in] what they do ... they're all adults ... I don't dictate to them.

Edward's relationship with his son sounded like the situation of two strangers who share a house:

My young fellow, he works from 4:00 [pm] to 12:00 [am], so we kind of pass in the night ... bump into each other a bit on the weekend, but otherwise ... we don't see one another.

Conversely, some of the widowers noted that they did not want advice from their children. Leroy, for example, whose daughter wanted him to move to a larger centre where he would be closer to a hospital, commented:

She wasn't ever protective, too, too much before because she knows I'm independent. And I don't like advice ... I shouldn't say I don't like advice. I analyse it, try to figure out who it's coming from.

Leroy's emphasis on his independence and autonomy was not unusual. The men worked to retain their status as adult men through resisting any attempts on the part of their children to influence their lives. They saw themselves as competent men who as fathers had been in charge and resisted any threats to this self-perception, particularly from their children (Siebert et al. 1999: 529).

Most widowers described a positive relationship with their children, whether it was emotionally close or not. There were, however, a few widowers whose descriptions of their children was explicitly negative. Several talked about children who had broken off contact with their fathers or with the whole family, while others found their children bothersome.

Edward, for example, has four children, three of whom keep in close touch, but one of whom does not keep in contact with anyone in the family. This daughter lives overseas and:

never has any written or any contact, so it's too bad, but I mean, there's nothing we can do about it.

Al, who had three children, was divorced from his first wife, remarried and then became widowed, has a close relationship with his daughter but commented that 'I haven't had a long-term relationship with the boys, just my daughter.' In both cases, the adult children had ceased communicating with their fathers and/or family before the men became widowed.

Bernie seemed to have a warm relationship with his children and was financially generous with them. His relationship had grown closer with his children since his wife's death, but:

> I'm a little cynical. I tend to feel that the closeness is because of my generosity toward them ... financially.

This uncertainty created a barrier between Bernie and his children. He did not feel that he could discuss this issue with them, even though there was no real evidence that their attentiveness was born of greed.

When their wives died, the widowers engaged in building routines that were no longer constrained by the existence of a partner. It is not unusual for both widowed men and women to find that their children do not like these changes and criticize them. The men saw these children, particularly daughters, as 'controlling and anti-change' (Wilson 1995: 111). This problem often involved emerging relationships with new women.

When the widowers had problems with daughters, they criticized their personalities. They found these daughters overbearing because they seemed to be trying to take over some components of the role of wife. Matthew, for example, got along quite well with his son but described his daughter, who disapproved of how he was living his life, as 'a nuisance' and 'a grump, a real grump ... [with] no sense of humour.' Similarly, Keith, whose daughters refused to meet the woman with whom he was involved, said:

> Well, the oldest girl, I find she's almost a nuisance, 'Dad, you shouldn't do this. Dad, you shouldn't do that.' ... I guess she's a bit like that.

Matthew and Keith were not only identifying children's interference in their lives, they were also observing a protectiveness that led their children to question their decisions. Like widows (van den Hoonaard 2001), widowers want their children to support them after their spouses' deaths, but they do not want their children to take over. After all, they are men. The next section deals with how the widowers talked about this issue.

'Checking Up on Dad'

Because research finds that adult children are often overprotective towards widows, I asked participants, 'some people find that their children become protective of them when they become widowed. Did you find that at all?' One-quarter of the men stated unequivocally that their children had not become protective, while about the same proportion stated that the children had been appropriately supportive, and 43 per cent replied yes. It is not only the positive and negative responses that matter, but also how the men framed their responses and the explanations they provided in support of their comments.

Izzy was, perhaps, the most emphatic in his statements about why his children were not protective:

> I was very self-sufficient, and I was pretty strict. I don't think that they felt that I needed protection ... I was the man of the family.

He used his role in the family in the past, I *was* the man and I *was* strict, to emphasize what he saw as the essential masculine place in his family. He maintained the same identity as the masculine father even though he was old and a widower.

Stan did not interpret his daughters' actions as protective per se, but the daughter who lives in western Canada is, 'always after me to go out west,' and his other daughter, who lives at home, loves gardening and 'always has me doing a lot of that which keeps me busy.' Stan's remarks illustrate that the boundary between being domineering and supportive may be in one's definition of the situation. A different man might define these approaches as intrusive, controlling, and threatening to his autonomy. A significant number of the men were, like Stan, very satisfied with the support they received from their children and did not interpret their actions as being overprotective. It was the men's definition of the situation, rather than what their children actually did, that resulted in whether the men interpreted the behaviour positively or negatively.

For some, the time-limited nature of their children's support and help made it possible for them to appreciate rather than resent it. Patrick, for example, was thankful for his children's 'rallying around' right after his wife died, but they treated him like the competent man he was and did not try to take over the decision-making.

In addition, the men knew that they would have to build new lives independently. Chad, for example, was grateful that his daughter stayed two extra weeks after his wife died but at the same time:

At that point, I wanted to get on with my life. I knew what I had to do, and I was almost anxious to get started at it. It had to happen ... So, I just wanted to get them first weeks in ... being alone.

Stephen, who was over 90 and the oldest participant in the research, had a strikingly different approach. His daughter took over many responsibilities after Stephen's wife died, and he regarded her doing this as appropriate. For example, he did not know how he had gotten enrolled in the Meals on Wheels program, but he suggested that perhaps his daughter had arranged it. Indeed, he remarked that, without his daughter, he probably would have become seriously ill. It is significant that Stephen described his daughter's role as being in loco parentis. Stephen was quite satisfied and seemed to take for granted, for the most part, that his daughter would be in this role. But, even he was concerned that she was going too far:

I sometimes think too much. Like, for instance, not allowing me to drive a car.

Checking up was another way that children showed their concern, although some fathers succeeded in discouraging this practice. Bob, for example, explained that:

Of course, they would, every once in a while, call or something. They couldn't find me or get a hold of me, which was natural that I would be gone somewheres. So one would call the other one, and then the other would try to call to see where I was. After awhile, they'd locate me ... But then ... they accepted that, you know, that I wasn't going to be in the house all the time, that I was an outdoors person.

Bob, by describing himself as an 'outdoors person,' invoked a central symbol of rural masculinity (Campbell et al. 2006) and reminded both me and his children that he was a real man.

Other men were less successful and resented their children's attempts to influence their behaviour. They valued their independence and did not want anyone telling them what to do. A few, like Keith, noted that their children disapproved of a wide range of decisions:

'Dad, you shouldn't' do this or that. I guess she's a bit like that, but the only real rift was when they found out I had a [woman] friend.

Keith and Matthew both have had considerable difficulty with their children's attitudes about their relationship with a woman, and the forcefulness of their reaction is likely directly related to this particular issue of contention.

A more common reaction was for the men to highlight a particular example of overprotection while still characterizing their relationship with their children as good or close. Winston, for example, is quite satisfied that his children call and check up regularly. When I asked about protectiveness, however, he recounted a story about the children's reaction to his undergoing medical tests:

> The only thing I encountered ... when I was sick last year. They didn't seem to think I would be able to face up to all these things ... They came around to see me, and they were very nervous. And they seemed to think, you know, that I'd collapse ... they were really worried. They didn't think I could face even the tests without a lot of help.

Mel is pleased that his daughter calls every day, but when I asked him if his children were overprotective or questioned his decisions, he recounted a story of becoming interested in a woman whom he had met on a trip to another part of the country. His child convinced him not to pursue a serious relationship with this particular woman because she was divorced. He commented wistfully: 'If only she'd been living around here.' She was the only woman who had interested him since his wife's death three years earlier, but he did not seem angry at his daughter's interference. He concluded: 'I guess she was just looking out for my affairs, eh?'

While these challenges reflect children's concerns with their fathers' safety or behaviour, some of the widowers related situations in which the difficulties were located in problems their children had. Their desire to recount these problems and the way the men described them come next.

Adult Children's Problems

The men's forthrightness in identifying and talking about their adult children's problems came as a surprise. It is notable because I did not ask them whether or not their children's lives were going well. I simply asked them how the relationship with their children had changed. The participants took the initiative to identify and focus on these situations in light of their becoming widowers. For the most part, participants' tones, when talking about their adult children's shortcomings were very matter-of-fact and unemotional. They, once again, used 'factual speech' (Kirsi et al. 2000) to become the objective observer of a situation over which they did not claim culpability or participation.

Several of the widowers commented that a child's less-than-satisfactory marriage affected their own relationship with that child. In some cases the marriages created a barrier, while in others the father was called upon to help out in some way, usually financially (Hoffman, McManus, and Brackbill 1987).

Like many older parents (Peters et al. 2006: 548), George saw his relationships with both a daughter-in-law and a son-in-law as problematic. These children-in-law did not live up to either the intellectual standard of this highly educated man or to his moral standard of being able to control one's drinking. Rejecting shallow alcoholics established George as the opposite kind of person, an insightful, self-disciplined man.

Fathers often see themselves as protectors of their daughters, and the participants who had divorced daughters were comfortable stepping into this role through helping financially. They were most satisfied if their relationship with their daughters reflected a measure of reciprocity and included traditional gender roles. Leroy, for example, had a satisfying, reciprocal relationship with his divorced daughter. He helped her financially, and she and her children did some chores that he would have trouble doing himself:

> She's divorced, and she has these two teenagers, and they love it [at my house]. And, of course, Grandpa looks after the grocery bills, and that helps them ... they're good, too. They do all the grass cutting, and all that type of stuff.

Tim also helped a divorced daughter financially, but his relationship lacked the reciprocity he had hoped for:

> I speak to her quite often on the phone. I gave her a ... phone card ... I helped her out all I could because her [financial] settlement wasn't all that good ... I've been diverting a lot of money to her, the last few years – for lawyers and things like that.

He felt pride that he was able to help his daughter but was disappointed that she was not willing to move back east just in case he needed her:

> If anything happens, I wouldn't have to go into a nursing home.

It is not surprising that Tim was disappointed. Many parents, although they prefer not to ask for help, expect their children to step in if needed (Peters et al. 2006). Particularly in the more traditional context of Atlantic Canada, men are likely to expect their daughters to conform to the obligations of familism.

Other participants identified children's psychological or emotional problems. Grant, for example, indicated that he was worried that his daughter seemed to be suffering from severe depression, whose source he located in the combination of her losing her mother and having a miscarriage in quick succession. Leonard and Marcel also identified children who were unable to deal with the loss of their mothers. Marcel had suggested that his son seek counselling but to no avail.

Al's son had a serious mental illness, and he explained that his children had not had any children because they were afraid the disease might be inherited. Al did what he could within the limits of what his son would allow, but did not overstep the boundaries his son established:

> I kind of help, support, him a little ... There's not much I can do for him medically, and then he doesn't let you do too much for him.

Samuel and Herbert both had children with life-long disabilities. Their approaches were quite different, because Samuel's daughter and son-in-law were physically disabled while Herbert had two children who had a developmental disability. Samuel's daughter and her husband's disability only came up in light of his having to:

> really take care of them [right after my wife died]. And get them food and set the table, and they stayed with me for a week.

Samuel's daughter and son-in-law lived independently and both had established careers.

Herbert and his wife, on the other hand, had a whole system worked out before she became ill with a degenerative disease, and their daughter and her husband were an integral part of that system:

> We hired our daughter and son-in-law to move up there [in a house nearby], and they take care of them ... They're still living in the other house, taking care of the kids.

Three men identified moral weakness or character flaws as part of their discussion about their relationship with those children, all sons. Ralph said of his son:

> He's not exactly a prime son ... in many ways. He's got a heart as big as all outdoors, but, beyond that, he has his weaknesses ... he's got a nice wife [but] he tends to want to play around with his second-hand goods.[2]

Some men criticized their sons for failing to achieve independence and to build stable families of their own, goals that Nydegger and Mittness (1991) have found that fathers have for sons. Thus, when Ralph talks of his son's unfaithfulness to his wife, he characterizes him as an inadequate son rather than a poor husband.

The participants' willingness to identify problems or character flaws of their children was striking. Also striking was their placement of blame, if any, outside of themselves. In particular, the men tended to blame their wives for character flaws of sons and personality issues with daughters. Edward, for example, has a daughter who moved to another part of the world to escape her domineering mother. His son, on the other hand would always:

> do what his mother wanted ... He kind of lived under her thumb ... So I've been trying to slowly kind of ... get him out on his own. I can't very well push the poor kid out if he's not used to it, you know.

Edward remarked that his wife always made excuses for his son and daughter, which he implied was the root of their problems. He also described another daughter who 'finally moved out west' after itching to get out from under her mother's influence.

This pattern is consistent with the practice of 'mother blaming,' in which, 'mothers [are blamed] for the actions, behavior, health, and well being of their (even adult) children' (Jackson and Mannix 2004: 150). It is not surprising, therefore, that some men's opinions would conform to the idea that their children's problems resulted from the mothering they received.

Most men, however, referred to their wives' relationship with the children in more positive ways to explain what their own relationship was like with those children after their mothers' deaths. The next section will explore this issue.

The Importance of Mothers

Six participants commented that their children had been very close to their mother. Bob suggested that his children were closer to their mother because they were girls while Charles simply said that his children were 'devoted to their mother.' Keith said:

> I don't have the grip on them that [she] had. I think that's the way with most mothers ... They don't come home as often as they did when she was around. Of course, she knew all the news, where their old friends from high school were and what they were doing. I'm not much for stuff like that, you know.

Keith is identifying his wife's place as kinkeeper of the family, a role that women have traditionally taken. The job often passes from one generation to the next, from mother to daughter (Rosenthal 1985: 972). Other men found that their children transferred their closeness to their fathers now that their mother was no longer there.

A number of the wives had entrusted their wishes to their children before their deaths, and this action had surprised some of their husbands. Patrick, for example, had been widowed twice. He had a pre-nuptial agreement with his second wife and, therefore, her children looked after her estate after her death. His first wife had told their daughter to 'be good to your father and invite him out and take care of him in that respect.' Patrick did not know about this communication until after his wife had died.

Jacob, Leroy, and Chad reported that their wives had told their children of their desires regarding either their funeral or the dispersal of personal items. For example, Chad's wife:

> wrote a little hand-written will with all her personal items ... It was to my son ... not to me. And she dated it and signed it ... We had a fireproof box for all our papers, and I found it in there.

Although it is possible that his wife wrote the will before she knew she was dying and, therefore, might have thought Chad would be likely to die first, he assumed that she had written the will with the knowledge of her impending death. Three years later, Chad still seemed hurt by the thought that his wife had entrusted her son with her wishes rather than him.

It became clear as I looked at what widowers said about their and their wives' relationships with their adult children that traditional roles related to gender played a key part in how they talked about and understood them. Their assumptions became specifically explicit when they talked about their daughters as *daughters*.

The Centrality of Daughters

Although the participants talked about both sons and daughters, daughters clearly played a more central role in their fathers' lives as widowers. This finding is not surprising and coincides with other re-search (see Connidis 2001). Both the men and their daughters appear to have taken for granted that the daughters would step in to help with a variety of tasks including disposing of their mothers' clothing, doing some cooking, providing emotional support, and kinkeeping.

Consistent with Moore and Stratton's findings in *Resilient Widowers*, a number of men depended on their daughters to go through their wives' things and arrange for them to be removed from the house. There does not seem to have been much consultation about this; rather it is simply what happened:

> And when [she] died, the kids moved in; my daughters moved in and separated everything ... (Patrick)

Some men wanted to make sure that their daughters had the opportunity to take anything they wanted that had belonged to their mothers, and this desire was part of the rationale for the daughters' going through the clothing:

> Anything my daughter wanted, she can have ... Otherwise it just went to the clothing bank ... I wanted to make sure anything she could use, she had the first chance at. (Mel)

A few widowers commented that their daughters came in so quickly that they hardly had time to hang onto anything themselves for senti-mental purposes. Izzy, for example, noted that:

> My daughter came down; my wife was a clothes hog. She had a closet stuffed. [My daughter] came down, and she took these 32-pound garbage bags and filled up 16 of them ... She took it to ... Goodwill. Gave it all away.

But I grabbed a couple of things. One is an old handbag. And one is a sort of blouse ... So when I go into the closet, I look at that, and I look at the handbag, an old handbag. [emphasis added]

In contrast, Matthew had expected his daughter to handle this difficult task, but gave up waiting for her to get around to it:

Yeah, it was hard with my wife's clothes. My daughter kept promising she'd come and pack them up and take them to the Salvation Army, and she never did. So I finally had to do it. And that was hard.

Clearly, Matthew had seen the responsibility for this task as naturally falling to his daughter.

Widowers' level of comfort with their daughters' behaviour relates to their perceived level of control. Mel made the decision regarding his daughter's getting the clothes she wanted while, in contrast, Izzy's daughter was in control. She simply swooped down and took over, leaving Izzy a few items as sentimental objects. Izzy repeated that he looks at a handbag several times to underline the poignancy of not having had the control to decide what he wanted to keep. Had he had the option, Izzy would have chosen a more sentimentally meaningful object than a purse. The differing interpretations result from a lack of norms regarding who should have been in charge.

Cooking is another area in which it seemed 'natural' for daughters to help, and six widowers specifically referred to some cooking that the daughters undertook. There were no daughters who took over all the cooking for their father.

Leonard, whose daughter was a teenager when her mother died and whose marriage entailed a traditional gender division of tasks, commented that his daughter began doing some of the cooking. He commented:

She was a student and needed to focus on school. And her inclination was to try to take care of us. So I think she tried to step into that role ... she and I would have arguments about that ... around who was going to do the mother stuff.

In contrast, Stan, whose adult daughter lived with him and was involved with a weight-loss program at the time, was quite comfortable letting his daughter take primary responsibility for the cooking:

> My daughter does a lot of the cooking. She's a good cook ... I usually eat
> what she cooks, and, of course, it doesn't do me any harm.

Other daughters took over more specialized cooking. Jacob's daughter, for example, visited her father in Florida and made Thanksgiving dinner for him and a few invited friends. Leroy's daughter does his home baking, often does his grocery shopping, and, when she visits, 'she rarely comes out without a casserole or something.'

Overall, the participants' comments about their daughters confirm traditional gender expectations. Several daughters' taking on the kinkeeping role that their mother had had was consistent. Marc, for example, explained:

> They're creating their own traditions now ... even though my daughter ...
> has attempted in her own way to invite her brothers and sisters and me to
> [her home]. And that, more or less, replaced what used to occur in the
> family home.

Chad's daughter's efforts to ensure that her brother called him on Father's Day also fulfilled the kinkeeping role.

Although the responsibility for carrying on family traditions primarily fell to daughters, one widower, Grant, whose wife had died the year before our interview, did note that:

> My son took over what used to be our duty [the year my wife died]. And
> that was to have a Boxing Day dinner and get together for the extended
> family.

Grant noted that he would be hosting Christmas at his house the year of our interview, and commented that hosting Boxing Day 'would be up for grabs' because his son and his wife wanted to do it again. It was unclear who would host Boxing Day that year. Because Grant was a widower, he was no longer the centre of family life. The torch may have been passed to the next generation regardless of Grant's wishes.

This chapter has shed light on the complex and diverse relationships that the widowers had with their adult children. Previous studies of intergenerational relationships have little to offer in thinking about these relationships because most researchers adopt the concept of 'support' or 'care' in advance of collecting and analyzing their data (Connidis 2001). These conceptualizations paint a picture of the older generation as passive recipients of their children's assistance. The men in my study rarely identified what their children did for them (or what they did for their children) as support or care. They appreciated the help and emotional support they received from their children right after their wives' deaths, but they did not express their ongoing relationships in either of these terms. Rather, they saw themselves as equal participants in reciprocal relationships. They gave as much as or more than they received and reacted strongly when they did not feel in control of their relationships with their children.

In addition, most studies that explore intergenerational issues focus on the perspective of the adult children. Peters, Hooker, and Zvonkovic's (2006) discussion of ambivalence in the perceptions of older parents' attempts to redress this omission, but all of the fathers in their study were married. There are some studies that look at how the change of marital status affects intergenerational relations, but these primarily look at divorce rather than widowhood (Connidis 2001), and the change of marital status is usually in the adult child's generation.

The gender of the children had a large impact on how the widowers interpreted their relationships with them. We have long known that daughters provide more care than sons and that those with daughters receive more help. In this chapter, unlike in previous studies (e.g., Ha et al. 2006), the sex of the adult child affected both the father's expectations and his interpretations of the child's actions.

Several of the fathers described closer relationships with their children and explained that in becoming closer they had sometimes encompassed the lost relationship with the mother who had played the role of both kinkeeper and comforter (Rosenthal 1985). It is the widowers' willingness to emphasize problems in their interactions with and feelings about their children that came as a surprise.

Of great interest are the areas of tension that the fathers depicted. The recent development of theoretical discussions around generational ambivalence sheds some light on these accounts. Luescher and Pillemer (1998) suggest that the concept of ambivalence would be useful in understanding the complexity of intergenerational relationships in response to the previous practice of analysing them in terms of solidarity or alienation with very little in the middle. They argued that families that experience high levels of solidarity would be very likely to contain dissatisfaction, struggle, and conflict as well.

Luescher and Pillemer's suggestion was timely, and others have since adopted the concept of ambivalence in the study of family relationships, notably Connidis and McMullen (2002), who observed that

those with more power in a relationship have more options in the negotiation of those relationships, while those with less power may resolve
any conflict through acquiescence. It is arguably the members of older
generations who have less power, particularly when they become widowed. These widowers did not accept this loss of power gracefully.

Because mixed feelings may reflect the lack of agreed-upon norms or
expectations in a relationship, times of status transition contain an increased potential for 'heightened ambivalence' resulting from 'murky'
expectations. (Luescher and Pillemer 1998: 423). This uncertainty means
that widowers' expectations regarding their relationships with their
children may be unmet because they had expected their interactions to
involve support and positive interactions. (Fingerman et al. 2004: 803).
These men's move from being married fathers to widowed fathers
made it challenging for the widowers and their children to negotiate
their identities and obligations successfully (van den Hoonaard 2003).

Peters, Hooker, and Zvonkovic (2006) have identified two areas in
the perceptions of aging parents about their relationships with their
children that may be problematic, and both are consistent with how the
widowers in this study talked about the relationships with their children. These areas include the busyness of the children's lives and the
fathers' reluctance to intrude on their children's personal lives by not
asking too many questions or by refraining from commenting on their
children's marriages, decisions, or behaviour.

The men who commented that their children were very busy or had
their own families to take care of fit into the first category. Their words
recognize the normative quality of this interpretation as well as a poignancy around feeling that they did not get to see their children enough.

Consistent with Peters, Hooker, and Zvonkovic's findings, most of
the men did not 'feel it was appropriate to interject their personal
opinions into every facet of their childrens' [sic] lives' (2006: 547).
This attitude was most obvious in the men's discussions of their children's marriages.

The most explicitly negative comments were associated with daughters, whom some widowers found overbearing or 'grumpy' in one way
or another. Some characterized their daughters' opinions about the
way they lived their lives as simply irritating (Fingerman et al. 2004)
while others sounded as if they truly disliked their daughters.

Nydegger and Mitteness (1991) suggest that daughters are less critical of their fathers than sons because they assess their fathers in terms of
family performance: 'Good traditional father-daughter relations are
based on uncritical, mutual affection to which incomprehension seems

to be no hindrance' (263). Perhaps this breaks down for some fathers and their daughters when the wife/mother dies. This is most likely to occur when the father has become involved with a romantic partner. Thus, the daughter's objections break the unspoken rule of uncritical, mutual affection and result in the father's strong reactions. These objections also challenge the identity of 'father,' which traditionally places the father at the centre and in charge of the family.

As well, some daughters adopted part of the traditional wife's role of monitoring their fathers' inclinations. These men reacted by describing their daughters as nagging, carping women who fit into the stereotype of the controlling wife. This stereotype is widespread and appears in the popular media in such humourous articles as 'Put a Cork in the Whine' (Haigh 1999), which refers to women's nagging as 'our calling' and offers tongue-in-cheek advice on how a man can put an end to his wife's nagging. When the widowers see their daughters as domineering, the relationship exhibits strong role conflicts. The women who should have been adoring daughters have disappointed their fathers by criticizing how they live their lives. Compared to sons who have not lived up to their father's expectations – a disappointment that does not elicit the same strength of reaction – domineering daughters appear as very negative characters, indeed.

Widowers' comments about their relationships with their sons contained less emotion, and more men commented on their sons' characters, in contrast with their daughters' personalities. Not surprisingly, negative comments were about a son's inability to become independent or, in one case, remain faithful in his marriage. This is consistent with Nydegger and Mitteness' observation that: 'a father's responsibility is to foster his son's independence and ensure the basis for his future in social and economic terms' (1991: 254).

In contrast, two daughters were divorced, and their fathers thought it completely natural to help them out financially whether by paying for lawyers or contributing to grocery costs.

Finally, we can see the conformity of many daughters' and fathers' expectations for gender appropriate behaviours. The daughters helped with disposal of their mothers' belongings, with cooking, by arranging for help (e.g., Meals on Wheels), and by providing emotional support for their fathers. The sons conformed to gender expectations by not appearing in their fathers' discussions of help following their wives' deaths, and the lack of any comments by those fathers that they should have provided assistance.

6 Women in the Lives of Widowers

One of the most ubiquitous stereotypes regarding widowers is captured in the phrase that upon becoming widowed, 'women grieve and men replace.' My interviews with widowers reinforced the commonly held belief that finding a new woman is an intrinsic part of widowhood for men. Indeed, issues related to remarriage or finding a woman companion permeated the interviews and arose in response to a variety of questions that asked men to talk about their experience as widowers; in general, what it is like living alone, and to comment on their relationships with their adult children. The men exhibited a desire to remain in control of the progression of their relationships with women, as well as a reluctance on the part of some to commit themselves to a particular woman. They made it clear that repartnering[1] of some sort is an inherent part of being a widower.

Scholars have suggested that finding a connection with a new woman is an indication of a man's successful adaptation to widowhood. Robert Rubinstein, for example, suggests that men seek social relations with women in response to 'the need for personal integrity' (1986: 32). He defines 'successful reorganization' for men who have been widowed as, 'the achievement of a life-style centered around a new relationship of intimate companionship with a woman' (Rubinstein 1986: 45).

Many of the participants presented in this chapter would certainly agree with this conception of successful reorientation. Nonetheless, the men's attitudes about repartnering were diverse, often ambivalent, and reflected beliefs about innate differences based on gender. Most of the men eschewed matchmaking except, as we shall see, the unique orientation of Samuel. The predominant desire of the men was to be in control of any decisions they made about connecting with women.

The next section will address the actual experiences the widowers re-count about their encounters with women. Here the cultural differences between the Jewish urban group in Florida and the more conservative, Christian group in Atlantic Canada are stark. The Floridian transplants were far more comfortable with women's taking the initiative in establish-ing a relationship than the Atlantic Canadians. As well, even though the Canadian men emphasized being in control over whom they connected with, their stories were lacking in detail and told with a minimum of agency.

Next, the chapter deals with cautionary tales about the trials and tribulations of getting involved with a woman too soon. Finally, the chapter talks about what the men said about their children's opinions and reactions to the possibility of their repartnering.

Attitudes towards Remarriage and Other Relationships with Women

Ambivalence towards marriage manifested itself in several ways. First, some men's dilemma was simply that they did not want to be either married or single. For example, Marcel, whose wife had died three years prior to our interview, frankly expressed his quandary:

> But I don't want to be alone. I don't want to. [But] I don't want to be remarried.

Marcel hoped to solve his difficulty by having a 'companion, a friend, a lady friend.'

George, who remarried within six months of his wife's death because he did not want to live alone any more,[2] and almost as quickly divorced, found himself afraid of making the same mistake twice. When asked if he had thought about remarriage after his divorce, he replied:

> Oh yeah, definitely. But with a contradiction. I also had a fear. I wanted to, but I was afraid ... very vulnerable ... if I developed an emotional attraction and emotional attachment to someone that I felt I had lost control ... be-cause that's what happened the first time [I married after my wife died].

Some men interpreted being single and being independent as syn-onymous and were, therefore, hesitant to commit themselves to another marriage. Keith, for example, thought about remarriage in terms of es-caping loneliness. He expressed hesitation about getting married be-cause marriage might intrude on his independence, which he associated with selfishness:

I don't know if I'll ever get married again ... It's a lonely life, but I'm enjoying my independence, too. You know, I can come and go as I please.

Similarly, Angus remarked that:

You get selfish being alone ... You know, it's nice, eh, I mean just the thought, 'hey, I'm hungry, it's three o'clock in the morning. I think I'll go get something to eat.' Well, if you were married, they'd say, 'Oh, you are crazy.' It's not that you'd go; it's the idea that you have the freedom to come and go. You don't have to answer to anybody. It's just you, and that's it.

Angus' reference to going out in the middle of the night is doubly ironic because, not only did he admit that he had no intention of actually acting on such an impulse, but it is also unlikely that he would have been able to find an open restaurant at that time of night, even if he wanted to.

These images of independence and autonomy symbolize the free life of the young bachelor. The implication is that giving up the freedom that accompanies the loneliness of widowhood through getting married or paired with a woman might lead to being managed in a variety of ways or being constrained. A new wife might inhibit Angus from eating that middle-of-the night sandwich or getting drunk. A wife may inhibit a man's 'natural,' that is, essentialized, masculine inclinations. The point is not that these widowers would actually get drunk or have a middle-of-the-night snack; it is that, as long as they are not married, they *could*.

Angus did comment that he might remarry, but that 'you would have to click.' He would not marry just to get married because, unlike some other men, he was 'quite self-sufficient' and did not want to get 'caught' or 'trapped' by marrying the first woman who came along.

Matthew, who was living with a woman, explained that:

Well, actually, I didn't want to get involved because it hurt so much at the time... and I was confirmed at that time that it's just not worth it.

In spite of feeling so strongly right after his wife died, he concluded, 'I guess it is – you have to have someone.'

In contrast to the uncertainty reflected in the ambivalent statements above, seven men had definitely decided against marriage but were interested in or had already found a woman to be a companion or a girlfriend. They were able to maintain their sense of freedom at the same time they claimed the masculine trait of heterosexuality. The most lighthearted explanation in this group came from Matthew, who replied to my observation that he and the woman he is living with are not married:

Oh no. She had fifty years of marriage. I had forty-two. She said, 'that's enough.' I said, 'good enough.' She doesn't want to get married again. And besides that, it's fun living in sin.

It is worth noting that Matthew credited his friend with not wanting to get married again. It may be that, had she wanted to remarry, he would have agreed.

Five of the men, three of whom were in a stable couple relationship with a woman, made it quite explicit that they felt having a companion is very important, but remarriage was out of the question. They all pin-pointed a connection with a woman as very significant. For example, Izzy, whose wife had died eight years before our interview, was 87. He made it quite clear that:

Nobody could live with me [because] I have my own ways, you know, and my own idiosyncrasies, my own crazy habits ... and I don't think anybody would tolerate *me*. [emphasis in original]

Izzy felt just as strongly that, 'I don't want to tolerate somebody else's nonsense either.' In spite of these obviously strong feelings against re-marriage, Izzy had been in a relationship with the same woman for five years, and when I asked him what the most important things are that other people should know about the experience of being a widower, he just as adamantly stated:

Try not to be alone ... Try not to be alone. Try to have a [woman] friend. Someone you can talk to. Someone you can confide in ... someone that you like to be with and not to be alone. Alone is the worst thing.

Bernie had a similar attitude. He had been a caregiver to his wife for many years and 'need[s] to be needed.' As well, his stable relationship gave him a 'connection' and allowed him to reconstruct that kind of lifestyle he had had when he was married. This included taking his woman friend on gambling trips to Las Vegas as well as introducing her to opera. Although his friend would have liked to live together, and Bernie considered their connection life-long and 'permanent,' he also had no interest in remarrying or moving in together:

I never want to lose my sense of independence.

Patrick also hesitated to think of remarriage because of the losses he had experienced. He had been widowed twice, the second time after just one and a half years of marriage.[3] He referred to what he called, 'that old saying: if you've had a good marriage, then you will look for a new mate.' Not surprisingly, since his experience with losing his second wife suddenly after such a short time, he had become more ambivalent about remarriage, but not about having a new woman in his life:

> If anyone came along that would strike me ... I might consider it ... Well, not even thinking of marriage that way. It'd be somebody I'd go out with. Yeah, I'd get back together in a relationship. No, I've thought of a relationship, but I haven't thought much of marriage.

Finally, Ralph, who was 77 and himself had a number of health problems, had promised his wife that he would never remarry. In addition to that promise, which he took very seriously, Ralph humorously described himself as a 'worn out old crock' who was 'on the downgrade.' As well, he had spent many years caring for his wife, who had had dementia, and was not willing to 'inherit' another set of health problems with a new wife who might have wanted to 'rearrange things [in the house] to her way.' In spite of all the reasons Ralph gave for not wanting to remarry, he was still interested in developing a relationship with a woman even though he thought it unlikely that he would succeed:

> So, actually, I'm on mission impossible. What I'm looking for is a reasonably attractive female ... who is willing to be my companion. She could stay in her place, and I'll stay in mine. And I haven't been kissed by a woman for so long, I'd probably have to do it sitting down because the shock might be too much for me ... If I were basically honest, yes, I'd love to be able to ... put my arms around a woman and kiss her like a woman should be kissed.

Ralph's ironic tone continued when I asked him at the end of the interview if he had anything he'd like to add. He laughingly said:

> No ... unless you're in the matching business or something [and] can find me a suitable female at a suitable age who doesn't want to get hooked up [i.e. married].

When we talk about the availability of people for older widows and widowers to marry, we often comment, as Kate Davidson (2004) does, that it is more feasible for men to repartner simply because there are so many more widows. However, we might see Ralph's comments as raising more abstract issues around feasibility. Davidson notes that men who remarry or repartner are younger, healthier, and wealthier. Combined with many men's desire to connect with a (sometimes much) younger woman who would not be as likely to be interested in them, repartnering may also lack feasibility.

Other men, who were not necessarily on the lookout for a long-term relationship, were definitely opposed to remarriage for other reasons. Ed, for example, had a very strong, supportive group of friends in his retirement community in Florida. They included him in their social activities so consistently that he said that his social life had not changed since his wife died. He, therefore, had no need of another woman:

> Because my friends have stuck by me, and I go out. I go out to eat in a group. I don't go out alone.

He, like Ralph, saw remaining single as a way of remaining loyal to his wife.[4] Deborah Carr (2004: 1065) has observed that, 'men who have high levels of social support from friends are no more likely than women to report interest in repartnering.' Ed's comments throughout his interview attest to his friends' filling his need for social activity and intimacy now that his wife was no longer there. This type of situation, however, is rare.[5]

Several participants were explicit about not being interested in women who were their own age. They did not find 'old' women attractive, and therefore, had no interest in spending time with them. Their hesitance in thinking about remarriage arose from their assumption that they would not be able to find a woman who was both interested in them and young enough to be attractive to them. The objectification of women in these rationales is striking and adds one more piece to the men's mosaic of masculinity. Note, in the following quotation, that Charles presumed that a five-year age difference was typical:

> I'm 75 years old, and ... what the hell. It's over. I know I shouldn't feel that way. I look pretty good. And in my mind, I can't associate with a 70-year-old woman. To me, a 70-year-old woman ... is an old lady. And I don't feel like going out with an old lady.

Jacob, at 83, was even more forceful in pointing out that his preference would be for a younger woman, 30 years younger. At the same
time that he recognized that a much younger woman would not be interested in a man his age, he stated unequivocally that women his age:

> are not that physically attractive any longer, you realize that.

Jacob also insisted that he was not willing to go to the effort that
building a relationship with a woman might entail. He credited his own
age with his assertion that he was not willing 'to hold the door for you
to get in the car' and go through all the work of developing a romantic
connection. Jacob recognized that his decision was contributing to his
continuing loneliness, but he argued that men who got involved were,
'grasping at straws or in our second childhood.' He, in contrast, was
realistic and recognized that 'you've got to take what you've got.' The
tenor of Jacob's remark was echoed by eight men in their discussions
about their potential to remarry. In essence, they were either not interested in or not willing to put effort into finding a new wife or companion; if it happened, however, it happened.

Others were not actively seeking or interested in remarriage, but they
were fatalistic. They used destiny speech to explain that they could not
be sure that they would not meet the right person; something would
click, and they would change their minds. Charles had only been widowed for seven months at the time of our interview. He said that he was
not interested in remarriage, but he remarked that:

> If some other lady kind of hit me, or I was attracted to her, or maybe if she
> was [similar to my wife], I might be interested ... because no one wants to
> be alone.

The Canadian men who are married or seriously involved with
women tell stories that have the same fatalistic flavour that we see in
Charles' comments.

Samuel was 83 years old and had been widowed for 6 years when we
spoke. He presented a picture that was diametrically opposed to the
practice of waiting to see what happens. Rather, Samuel described a
situation of desperation that some of the other widowers criticized. He
was, 'forced against my will,' to make dates because he was not interested in making friends with men and had found life 'meaningless'
when he was alone. Samuel stated several times that he had been reluctant to start dating and not ready, but he had found life so difficult after

his wife died that he averred no fewer than five times that he had had 'no choice' but to look for a new woman:

> So, you know, I had a lot of ladies to choose from and I did it reluctantly. I had no choice ... Otherwise I would have done nothing in the evenings. And I really couldn't stand the evenings when I had nothing to do. [Uh-huh] I don't mean nothing to do. I, I always could do something ... playing the piano in my own house ... reading books. After awhile, you get tired of reading. So, the only solution was to just go out with someone, and, you know, see what happens.

Samuel described only solitary activities as alternatives to getting involved with a woman. His desperation led to a number of misadventures, some of which were 'extremely interesting, even funny.' Samuel finally found a new woman, now his wife.

In addition to personal accounts of why they were or were not interested in remarriage, several men provided explanations that were more explicitly based on sex or gender differences between men and women. George, identifying one facet of the foundation of hegemonic masculinity – objectification of women – referred to men's 'slavery to testosterone.' He suggested that, as a result, men are 'always on the lookout for a member of the opposite sex, even when they don't know it.'

Keith, who was involved with a woman, raised two issues directly related to gender. First, his children were afraid that he might remarry, and they apparently believed that it was okay for a mother to remarry but not a father. It seems that the issue is that the father should not force the children to have a new mother even though Keith's youngest child was already in university when his mother died and would not have needed looking after.

The second item involved his own desire to have a long-term relationship. He explained that his children wanted him to get new furniture, but:

> I'd rather have a lady my own age making the choices ... [because] when [my wife and I] went, a house is just to me, is just, uh, when we went shopping, and she'd say, 'what do you think?' I'd say, 'You have better taste than I have, you know. Whatever you want.'

Ralph also thought a woman would want to pick out furniture, but this observation was a reason for him not to get involved. Interestingly, one of George's complaints about his second wife, whom he divorced, was that she insisted that they bring her furniture into his house and get rid of his. Making a home through choosing the interior decorations is a female-typed task.

In spite of all the ambivalence and hesitance that the men expressed in their interviews, many have either remarried or developed a serious relationship with a woman. Three were either married or engaged at the time of the interview. Three had remarried and divorced after being widowed, and two had remarried and been widowed a second time (including one man who had been widowed, divorced, and widowed again). In addition, one participant was living with a woman common-law, and five men had long-term romantic relationships that they considered permanent. In other words, half of the participants either were or had been connected with a woman after being widowed. Some of the men had met the women on their own while others talked about their relatives' and friends' attempts to match them up with a new woman.

Matchmakers

The men reported having had mixed attitudes towards and experiences with matchmaking. Some talked about extensive and intrusive attempts of others; some talked about matchmaking in more neutral terms, and finally, one man, Samuel, was grateful to people who attempted to connect him with a new woman.

A variety of people acted as matchmakers, and, for the most part, widowers were either not interested or resented their efforts. George, for example, said that his family did not want him to be a, 'lonely, old widower' and went so far as to arrange people for him to meet. George stated emphatically that:

> There was no way that I was going to allow my family to dictate who I was going to be relating to in any way, at any level.

Other men talked about people who told them about someone who seemed to be interested in them. Two had specific women referred to them by their daughters (Angus and Bernie).

Two men explained that they had been shocked that people had approached them either when their wife was still alive or right after her death. Matthew reported that:

I even had one lady say to me that she had a friend that she was going to introduce me to once my wife had passed away. And I thought, 'holy mackerel'!

In contrast, because he felt so desperate to get together with a woman, Samuel had the opposite reaction to people's matchmaking efforts. He commented that he was 'grateful' because he found that:

> The ladies I met who were recommended ... the experiences with them were much more pleasant than when I could meet these ladies cold [because] ... we had somebody in common.

In the end, Samuel did, indeed, meet the woman he eventually married through the efforts of a matchmaking friend.

A few men were not sure if people had tried to match them up or not. They claimed that they had not really noticed. For example, when I asked Leonard if anyone had tried to introduce him to women, he, at first, said no although he felt they were supportive of his going out. After thinking about it for a couple of minutes, he observed that there might have been some people who had been trying to fix him up but that he had been unaware of it if that's what they were trying to do.

Fending off matchmakers allowed the men to retain control. Some men, however, had problems in their actual encounters with women. Misunderstandings or fear of women's misunderstanding their intentions characterized several widowers' stories about situations involving women. Others were more concerned about changes regarding dating behaviour in the years since they had previously been single.

Encountering Women

At the most basic level, several widowers were worried about leading women on or giving them the wrong idea about their intentions.[6] Keith, who was involved in a steady relationship, recounted a few occasions when he had invited a woman for a drive or dinner without expecting it to lead to anything more than an evening out. Things got out of hand:

> Now I got myself in an awful mess ... Where I go down to my canoe, there's a lady always sitting out, and she's a separated woman ... So I just asked her if she wanted to go for a drive, one night, you know ... one thing leads to another. And the first thing I know, I started taking her out. And

then when I tell her that I already have a friend, she starts crying, and oh dear.

Keith told another story with a similar plot. In both stories, he made the 'mistake' of inadvertently giving a woman the impression he was more interested in her than he was, and one thing just seemed to lead to another. Keith's belief in his lack of intention or culpability in these situations was explicit.

In other situations, the men thought they had made it clear that they were not interested in a serious relationship, but the women unintentionally or intentionally misunderstood. Angus, for example, attended community dances where he:

> gives [the ladies] all a little dance ... everybody, you know, so you kind of dance and chit chat.

One woman, however, told Angus that she would like someone to be a companion, a dance partner, 'just someone to go out to supper [with].' After awhile, the woman wanted a deeper connection:

> Well, after awhile, she wanted more than that, and I wasn't interested ... she was quite annoyed ... She made the rules so I was staying with them, for that was the agreement I wanted.

Marcel worried about misleading women and inviting gossip. Marcel's and Angus' comments alert us to the potential challenge in trying to establish and maintain dyadic, cross-gender friendships (Adams 1985).

Other men told stories of women who were quite aggressive in seeking a relationship that was more than the men wanted. In this type of story, we get a picture of predatory women against whom men have to protect themselves. Herbert, for example, was not averse to remarriage but was only interested in 'Christians.'[7] He reported having difficulty convincing a particular woman that he really was not interested in her:

> But there's one widow that's sort of interested in me, but I'm not interested in her. And I told her, 'Look, to be honest with you. I don't want to lead you on.' And I knew she had [been] interested in me. And I told her, 'Look, we'll never be a couple so don't waste your time with me.' ... But she still calls every once in a while, calls me at least every day. And, but I told her, 'Look, you're wasting your time.'

This particular woman insisted that she just wanted someone to talk to, but Herbert was sceptical.

During our interview, Herbert did a lot of joking about widows and that he made sure they understood that they were not a couple. He also mentioned a widow who had suggested a purely sexual relationship. Herbert painted a picture in which he, as one of the few widowers around, was in great demand and continually had to fend off advances from lonely widows.

Herbert was not the only widower to give this impression. Matthew described his experience in response to my asking if anything had surprised him about his experience as a widower:

> Yes, about a month after my wife passed away. [The town I lived in] ... is a small village of about 350 people, and I swear, 200 of them are widows – all living alone. So the 'casserole brigade' started, and I hate casseroles. So I had ... a commercial freezer full of casseroles ... And [they] would start pounding on the door. That kind of frightened me.

John Bayley in his memoir, *Widower's House* (2001), also referred to 'the casserole brigade' in the opening sentence. He recounted the story of a woman's knocking on his door with a casserole in her arms, and commented that she was his first encounter with the 'casserole brigade.'[8]

Mel's comments combined the phenomenon of fear of misleading women with the experience of receiving unwanted attention:

> I've really learned that widows are lonely and they're really looking for a man ... if you said the wrong thing. If you've said anything at all, it might make them think that ... you're maybe interested in them. And, that, uh, you'd better watch out.

And:

> There was one woman that was calling so much that I actually put a phone [caller] ID ... Because I just couldn't seem to get away from her.

Mel went on to recount his experience in a square-dance group where he met another woman who was 'trying to be extra friendly.' This particular woman was so insistent that Mel 'dance with her all the time,' that, 'I stopped going to the group.'

These accounts, although they were all provided by men in Atlantic Canada, evoke the 'urban legend' prevalent in Florida retirement communities of the 'casserole ladies' (Moore and Stratton 2002: 146; van den Hoonaard 1994, 2001) who wait like vultures to descend on newly widowed men (Kingston 2007). Moore and Stratton quote one of the widowers whom they interviewed as suggesting that men who believed they were being pursued were 'fantasizing' while John Bayley (2001: 45-6) has written about his own sense of being chased by women:

There was really no need to feel threatened and disquieted. No doubt widowers' weakness, as it might be called, was a well-known phenomenon in circles which widowers – and perhaps widows, too – frequented. They misunderstood the kindness women bestowed on them in their trouble. They became inordinately vain, as if with an occupational disease. Pathetic really.

It is not only men who are of the opinion that widows lay siege to new widowers. One widow in Florida explained that if you bring a casserole to a widower while he is sitting *shiva*, it is too early. But, if you wait until *shiva* is over, you will be too late – some other woman will have already gotten the man.[9]

These observations, however, beg the question of whether or not men's perceptions of being the target of lonely women are correct. Studies demonstrate that most older widows claim that they have little or no desire to remarry while widowers are both more likely to say they are interested in remarriage and to actually remarry (Davidson 1999, van den Hoonaard 2001). In Canada, overall, men make up only 18 per cent of widowed people (Statistics Canada 2004). In other words, if half of widows do not want to remarry, that still leaves slightly over two widows for each widower. It is not surprising that widowers sometimes feel besieged by the numbers of single women around them.

But it is easy to see how practical circumstances can lead men to misunderstand the intentions of women. Some women may simply think that they are being helpful. One widow, whom I interviewed for an earlier study (van den Hoonaard 2001), commented that she enjoyed baking pies and bread and would have liked to give them to men who were single. She found, however, that some men misunderstood her purpose and fled because they believed she was 'after them.' Similarly, Laurel Richardson (1985) noted in her book, *The New Other Woman*, that men think that women who make eye contact with them are signalling sexual attraction while the women may be unaware of sending such messages. The likelihood of misreading motivation is great and limits the potential for comfortable cross-sex friendships among single older men and women.

Getting Together

Although the above discussion might give the impression that widowers were averse to new relationships, about half the widowers were married, living with a woman, in a permanent relationship with a woman with whom they were not living, or had married and then divorced or been widowed after their first wife had died. It is to the experiences of these men that we now turn.

Cultural differences between the Floridians and Atlantic Canadians were quite evident in the men's stories about how they got together with their current wife or 'friend.' The men from Florida lived in the social context of a retirement community where leisure activities and going out to dinner are quite prominent and women are more assertive (van den Hoonaard 1992). The men from Atlantic Canada are much more conservative and religious, and live in a social context that is much more work-oriented and age mixed, and where people are more indirect in communicating. The men interviewed in Florida are all Jewish, while only one of the men in Atlantic Canada did not identify with some denomination of Christianity.

Four of the eight widowers from Florida had a 'friend' at the time of our interview – one, Samuel, has since married the woman he was with when we spoke. Three of these men told stories that included assertiveness, or taking the first step, on the part of their girlfriend that is reminiscent of the stories that the Atlantic Canadian widowers recounted about being pursued by women and receiving unwanted attention. Cultural differences likely explain the men's different interpretations and reactions to the women involved.

Al, for example, met Esther at the clubhouse in his community about five years after his wife had died. As he recounted it:

> So one day, she was sitting in the clubhouse talking, and I was looking at her. And I said [to myself], 'She's not a bad looking woman.' I said, 'She might be tough' [because I overheard her arguing with someone over a hand of cards], but she's nice. She wouldn't be bad company for dinner.' So I walked over and I asked her if she'd like to go out to dinner.

The initial approach came from Al, but Esther soon took the initiative:

> After, she decided that she liked me ... She came over a lot more than I realized. I didn't mean to make a regular routine of it. I just asked her out once; and before I knew it, here she's coming in like she's my girlfriend. It's very ... actually, she pushed herself into it.

Al credited Esther with 'pushing' him out of his mood of 'being reticent about ... having a good time' that he had been in for the five years following his wife's death.

Izzy told a story about the woman who helped him out after surgery. Because these migrants to Florida usually do not have children or other family locally available, they often depend on friends for help. Ruth's initiative astonished Izzy:

> And the reason we became very good friends was, it's an amazing situation ... I had to have heart surgery. And after, I had a nurse part time. But at night, I was alone ... [Ruth] slept in another room in case I needed something at night. For two weeks. Until I was able to get on my feet. Well, that made quite an impression, so we became very good friends [i.e., a couple] ... Well, [the relationship] was on the way to becoming a nice relationship, [but] that really clinched it. And I would do anything for her now, you know. Because of the interest when I really needed it.[10]

The forwardness of the women who have become partnered with these Florida widowers was not off-putting in the same way it would have been to the men in Atlantic Canada. These Jewish, urban men were not as worried about being in control over whom they got together with as the Canadian group, and they were more comfortable with women's growing assertiveness as they age (Ginn and Arber 1995; Sinnott, 1977 cited in Keith and Brubaker 1979: 48).

As well, three of the four Florida widowers were involved in permanent 'living apart together' (LAT) relationships. LATs are 'lasting intimate relationships which do not include a mutual home; that is, an alternative to different forms of cohabitation' (Karlsson and Borell 2004: 2).[11] It is unclear whether or not these couples were physically intimate, but the connections were definitely romantic, exclusive, and permanent. This phenomenon had not reached Atlantic Canada at the time of the interviews, at least among the older population, in any significant way.

Except for Samuel, the Jewish men did not want to marry or live with their girlfriends. Bernie, for example, described Frieda as a 'sheer delight for me'; but when she suggested that they live together, Bernie interpreted her desire as a search for 'down-the-road security.' He recounted the conversation:

> She said, 'why can't we live together?' ... I should have been quite forthright with her and told her because I don't want to. I never want to lose my sense of independence ... and she pouted. And she touched on it for several days after that, and then it no longer had any currency. We just gave up on it ... It never mattered again ... She felt I was pretty well committed to her, and she didn't need that kind of reassurance.

Izzy noted that Ruth had hinted about living together but he simply made believe he did not understand what she was getting at.[12]

The Atlantic Canadian widowers, for the most part, were much more vague about how they got together with their new girlfriend or wife. They used phrases like, 'and then one thing led to another' to describe the development of their connections. Keith's story of meeting his woman friend while waiting for a tour guide at a boardwalk is characteristic:

> And there's this lady next to me, and I asked her how long the board walk was ... And she was kind of chatty, got talking to her ... it sounded like her husband was something like my wife; they're both very active in the community ... So one thing led to another.

The stories the men told about the development of relationships are notable once again for the lack of agency on their part. We might see this way of recounting the story as a form of 'destiny speech' – being at the mercy of forces that are beyond one's control (Kirsi et al. 2000). The vague way the men described how one thing led to another contradicts some researchers' assumptions that older men and women consider decisions about getting together carefully. De Jong Gierveld, for example, suggests that: 'In meeting potential new partners, older widowed ... women and men have to weigh carefully the pros and cons of the situation to be expected against the situation in which they currently find themselves' (2004: 88). We do not get the impression from these widowers that they adopted such a rational approach to their new relationships.

Matthew, the only widower who was living with a woman without marriage, met Janet on the street. He simply said that they 'got to talking.' After being formally introduced by a neighbour, Janet invited Matthew in for tea. A week later, they decided to live together. Matthew remarked, 'I don't fool around.' Matthew was repeating what he had done when he met his wife; they had married two months after their first meeting.

Cautionary Tales

Most of the men who had gotten together with women after their wives' deaths described successful relationships. However, three men remarried quickly, within one year, and all three marriages ended in divorce. Two of the men, Marc and Winston, blamed the haste with which they married for the demise of their second marriage while George blamed the divorce on his second wife.

George, whose wife had been in a nursing home for the four years preceding her death, described his reaction to his wife's death as having, 'almost an obsession to get involved.' He brought up the subject of his unsuccessful marriage before I had asked a single question:

> But after [my wife died], I decided that I don't want to live alone any more, and by pure chance, I met this woman who had been an old girl-friend. Our paths hadn't crossed for twenty-five years. And, somehow, I guess I thought the flame was still burning and, to make a long story short, within six months after my wife's death, I remarried. *Big mistake!* [emphasis in original]

George told of how his second wife had insisted that they use her furniture and even renovate his house to her liking. She also moved to Atlantic Canada from another part of the country. His paintings went into storage and, in the end, he paid for her move back to where she had come from. He rhetorically asked, 'See what a fool I was?'

In contrast, Marc and Winston credit their having gotten together with women too soon for the failure of their second marriages. Marc, in response to my asking him to tell me about his experience as a widower, replied:

> It was terribly lonely. It was depressing ... I too quickly began looking ... until such time as I recognized the fact that six months after [my wife's]

death, I had begun seeing my second wife ... It was much too premature, there is no question about it. I wasn't ready for it, but it was great to have a replacing love and affection and presence, this type of thing. But I hadn't given myself enough time to grieve.

Marc had begun seeing his second wife, someone who had been a student of his many years before, three months after his wife's death. Even at the time of the interview, Marc still had not worked out satisfactorily in his own mind how long a man should wait before getting romantically involved:

The problem arose, as it were, well it's too soon, but ... when is it right for me to remarry? And that became the issue as opposed to, well, it's too soon. Will two years do? Will three years do? I mean, am I supposed to wear widows' leaves or the black crepe on my arm – for how long? And, if I'm going to allow somebody else to decide for me, well, my God almighty, I might be grieving until the day I go to my grave.

Marc made the above comment in response to my asking how his children felt about his early remarriage. The quote demonstrates the absence of clear norms as well as this man's desire to decide for himself at a time that was, in his own words, too soon.

Children's Reactions to Their Fathers' New Relationships

Just as the widowers had different ideas about relationships with women, so did their children. Some men suggested that their children either thought their fathers should not remarry or get involved with a new woman while others thought it was a good idea and encouraged their fathers. Most of those men who were not currently involved with a woman opined that their children would not have a serious objection if the situation were to arise.

Some children thought their fathers were getting involved with another woman too soon while some widowers thought their children would never approve of anyone they brought home. Matthew, for example, described several instances when his children had objected to his being associated with a woman, at least partly because of the gossip involved. His daughter was upset that he went to the New Year's party following his wife's death. She objected to his going at all, but when a woman flirted with him at the party:

> Word got back to my daughter before I even got home. She was quite per-
> turbed about that. She said, 'You shouldn't carry on like that in public.' I
> said, 'Look, I've never done anything to be ashamed of, and I've never
> tried to tell you how to run your life; don't tell me at 60-some-odd years of
> age how to run my life.'

In this situation, there was no real connection between Matthew and
the woman at the party. The problem revolved around his explicit claim
of being attractive to women rather than his getting involved in an actual relationship.

Matthew's daughters objected to the relationship he did develop later,
and their attitude was the hardest part of his life related to the death of
his wife. They still objected to his relationship with Janet at the time of
the interview and referred to her as a 'witch.' Matthew remarked:

> I figure they want me to go up every day and stand at my wife's grave ...
> and weep and cry and come home and sit in my chair in the living room
> and go back the next day and do the same ... They think Dad couldn't ...
> get on with his life after their mother was gone, and I don't know what
> they expected of me.

Matthew's anger at his children came through in his interview, and he
clearly decided that his children were not going to decide the matter for
him. He and Janet continued to live together.

Keith felt that he was caught in the middle: being pressured by his
children, especially one daughter who refused to meet his new girlfriend, on one side, and by his friend who was pushing him to get
things settled with his children, on the other:

> Like two (of my children) are quite vehement ... Maybe I'm too easygoing
> ... Probably at the beginning, if I just had of walked in on them, you know
> ... but instead I told them.

Keith wondered aloud if his children might have accepted his girlfriend
if she had had more education. He had been optimistic at first that his
friend and children would enjoy each other:

> At the very beginning, I thought she would mix well. Because she's out-
> going and chatty and cheery and enthusiastic ... But she never got the

chance. And then again, she's the type, she's putting pressure on me all the time. She wants to meet them and thinks I'm not trying hard enough.

In contrast, other men felt supported by their children and even encouraged to develop a new relationship with a woman. Bob stated simply that his children saw his new wife as 'just another mother,' while Patrick reported that he had avoided any financial complications with a prenuptial agreement and, at his second wife's funeral, her children had commented positively that she had acted like a teenager again when they had gotten together.

The Florida widowers were more consistently confident that their children had supported or would support them if they became romantically involved with someone. In several cases, the children encouraged their fathers to find someone 'to go out to dinner with' (Izzy) or 'just for the sociability' (Ed). Note that in these two cases, the children may not have been thinking about another marriage for their fathers. Samuel, however, has remarried, and his children were also supportive:

> I don't think there is any great problem there ... I think they were even glad that their father had met somebody. They were very understanding.

In contrast to Keith, Samuel, while appreciating his children's acceptance of his new relationship, made it clear that it would not have mattered what they thought. He remarked:

> No, I never ask them anything. I never ask them anything about dates. I would just tell them, and they would look at me and smile.

Bernie's daughter was so interested in his meeting someone that she actually introduced him to a woman friend of hers. Although his children encouraged his getting involved, he felt that they were a little disappointed that he ended up with Esther, because of her disability. They commented, 'well, you've got to keep looking,' but Bernie was quite happy with Esther and had no intention of ending their relationship just to please his children.

In this chapter, we have seen how men's 'definition of the situation' affects their interpretation of women's behaviour. They believe that widows are desperate and that they are very attractive to these love-starved widows. They, thus, interpret every gesture on the part of women as an invitation or even pressure to form an exclusive, romantic relationship. For some, this results in their fleeing the women they define as predatory.

The different cultural contexts result in the men's interpreting women's behaviour differently. The Florida widowers are Jewish and are much more comfortable with women's assertiveness. They initiated their relationships, but in every case but one, the women increased the intensity of the relationship. The Atlantic Canadian men focused more on being in control, but they were also more likely to use 'destiny speech' (Kirsi et al. 2000) as they had when they were describing their wives' decline after being diagnosed with a terminal illness. When talking about their relationships with women, these men suggested that they made the initial approach; but then 'one thing led to another,' and they found themselves married.

Most of the men were open to the idea of a new relationship with a woman whether as a wife or companion. They defined developing a relationship with a woman as an intrinsic part of being widowers. Thus, they mentioned the necessity of deciding about remarriage in response to the very general, first question of the interview and in response to a variety of questions on other topics. Their ideas conformed to notions of masculinity that define being a real man as always being interested in or involved with a woman.

Nonetheless, there was diversity in the ways that the widowers talked about their opinions regarding remarriage. Their discussions covered their feelings of ambivalence about remarriage, preference for a companion or girlfriend over marriage, and fatalism with regard to the possibility of meeting a new marital partner. In addition, several men provided explanations based on beliefs about gender for their understanding about their and other men's desires to get together with a woman.

Developing a relationship with a woman entails overcoming ambivalence, finding ways to reach an understanding regarding the nature of the connection, and sometimes dealing with disapproval from one's children. Even so, half the men had managed to establish a connection with a woman most satisfactorily.

The uncertainty the men expressed about their relationships with women is echoed in the ways scholars conceptualize these connections. Alinde Moore and Dorothy Stratton (2002; 2004), for example, provide perhaps the broadest concept to characterize these relationships. They suggest the phrase, 'current woman,' to encompass the variety of shapes a widower's association with a particular woman might take. They write: 'A current woman is one who takes over at least some of a deceased wife's role, or does something beneficial for the man that his wife had stopped doing, or perhaps had never done. The relationship is some enduring combination of practical help, friendship, and companionship. Many relationships include intimacy which may or may not include sexual behaviour' (Moore and Stratton 2004: 122).

Thus, the term fits many types of connections from those involving remarriage to an adult daughter's accompanying her father to a social event so that he will have a 'date.'

Nan Stevens, in her Dutch study, uses the expression, 'steady companionship,' which she describes as a: 'Cross-gender relationship [that] involves regular companionship in a variety of activities ... Participants in steady companion relationships had difficulty labelling their partner; the other is referred to as a 'special friend,' a 'kind of girlfriend,' ... Most of these relationships are long-term, having lasted for several years, and involved a clear commitment to maintain joint activities and involvement. Feelings of affection are expressed more often than love ... Often participants in this type of relationship were previously acquainted' (2004: 56).

The connections that the widowers in Florida had with their 'friends' perhaps best exemplify steady companionship. The men communicated a strong commitment to those relationships at the same time as they underlined their reluctance to remarry or live with the women with whom they were involved.

Robert Rubinstein refers to a woman's filling the role of 'intimate companion,' who is: 'A woman of the same age range who acts as a confidante, with whom a man has a special, subjectively placed bond, and with whom he does things ... [the relationship] may not be sexual and may not be marriage-oriented but may exist as a relationship separated out by its specialness ... [It] allows [one to have] a relationship of friendship or a marriage-like tie and yet maintain an independent life-style' (1985: 64).

Rubinstein's choice of words emphasizes the opportunity to have emotional closeness with someone, and he believes such a relationship is necessary in order for a widower to reorganize his life and avoid a life that is 'independent of close association' (58). Several widowers, Marcel, in particular, would surely agree with this assessment.

Potentially complicating the development of a relationship that fits with any of these concepts is the challenge of negotiating with one's adult children. The widowers needed to wait long enough after their wives died so as not to invite either gossip or disapproval from their children, particularly daughters. As well, they needed to navigate the meeting of their new 'friend' and their children. For some widowers, particularly, the Florida group, this process seemed to go fairly smooth- ly with children who were geographically removed and encouraged them to find someone to go out with. The situation in Atlantic Canada was more complicated and diverse ranging from some children's refus- ing to meet their father's new romantic interest to some who, at least in the opinion of their father, saw the new wife as 'just another mother.'

The next chapter rounds out this part of the book which explores rela- tionships. It covers what men said about their relationships with friends.

7 Relationships with Friends

Friendship is one of those areas in which we often think of women as the specialists, and thus, there is very little understanding of the nature and process of older men's friendship. The research that does exist identifies men's reliance on their wives for friendship, the lack of intimate connections with friends, the things that inhibit men's forming close friendships, and, to a greater and greater extent, friendship in terms of social support (Adams 1994, Moore and Stratton 2002). Men, according to Powers and Bultena (1976), often rely on their wives to make friends, are dependent on their wives for emotional intimacy, and do not make time in their lives for male friends (Tignoli 1980). Moreover, men's friendships are often premised on shared activities. Paul H. Wright (1982) characterizes this tendency as side-by-side relationships in comparison with face-to-face friendships among women. Finally, friends are usually about the same age, and most people see cross-gender friendships as always potentially romantic (Matthews 1986: 93).

Similar to widows, widowed men report both losing some friendships and feeling uncomfortable with couples. Also similar to widows, men believe that the problems they have maintaining friendships result from their belief that many of their friends had really been friends with their wives rather than with both of them. This often stems from the loss of the friendship: it is impossible to know if they are correct in their assumption or are redefining the nature of the relationship in an effort to understand the decline of these friendships.

There are important differences in how the widowers talked about friends. Several explained that they had not needed friends outside of their marriage, while others said that their wives had been responsible for initiating contacts with friends. A number of men pointed out that they had lost a significant number of friendships through death and illness. A few of the men identified themselves as loners and explained that they had never had many friends, which they did not see as a problem.

In contrast to the men who reported a loss or lack of friends, some men did talk about people who had been very supportive. One widower from Florida provided a striking example that he, himself, recognized as an anomaly. His discussion about his friends provided a description of what a rich, supportive friendship network looks like at the same time he contrasted it with the more common widowhood experience.

Loss of Friends Is Natural: You Just Drift Away

Eleven of the widowers talked about a decrease in the number of friends as if it were gradual, natural, and not very significant. These men did not express disappointment with the friends who had drifted away. Keith, for example, took some responsibility for the demise of friendships:

> It was a kind of a gradual thing. I don't blame them. I just probably haven't followed up on it, you know. You just sort of drift away, so to speak.

Winston also saw the diminution of friendships as natural and, perhaps, a part of getting older:

> Some, I don't see. I don't mix with them as much ... that's just as much me doing that as them ... When you get older, something often happens to one of your friends ... We were close to one couple, but I am, I don't mix with them as much, anything like as much as we used to. But the husband, he's been quite sick.

Chad seemed bemused by my questions about his relationships with friends and noted that single people do not frequent the same places as married people:

> We had some friends that we used to go visiting all the time. I don't know. I just, I've heard it said and maybe I just let it happen, that when you're single, you don't go to the same places you do when you're married. I don't think it's any kind of put down for anybody ... But it just doesn't happen. I guess I don't know why.

Chad's reaction to my question about friends suggests that he had not given much thought to the issue. Others provided more concrete explanations.

The Odd Man Out

Related to the above comments and appearing explicitly in the interviews of five men was the idea that for a single man, it is awkward to be around couples. The widowers constructed this situation as feeling like a fifth or third wheel and the odd man out:

> I supposed it's the case that you're the odd person out there, the odd man out sort of thing. (Stan)

> You're sort of like a third person out ... You don't fit in now with couples like you used to. (Herbert)

> I think they're a little uncomfortable with me ... I turn up and I'm like a fifth wheel ... you kind of felt that you was the odd person out ... You know, that two's company, but three makes a crowd ... you'd be the odd person. Go somewheres ... and maybe there'd be a couple or maybe three couples going – well, you made seven. (Bob)

The prevalence of the terms 'fifth wheel' and 'odd man out' underscores the two-by-two nature of socializing among and with couples. I heard those two phrases so many times that I would suggest that they have become clichés.

Bob also wondered if people were inviting him along because, 'they thought you was alone.' Bob's reaction to this feeling and to the awkwardness he felt as a single man among couples was to turn down invitations when he thought he would be the only person there who was not half of a couple:

> Sometimes, a lot of time, you know, they was going to be all couples ... you just kind of declined. And not make it odd or awkward for them as well as yourself.

Four men explained that they were no longer receiving invitations to social events as they had in the past. Conrad said that he:

> Suddenly realized that once upon a time, we, as a couple, were invited to a great deal of functions, and alone, the invitations ceased completely. Oh yes, yes.

Two widowers from Florida also noticed this disappearance of invitations to social events. When I asked Jacob how his life had changed since his wife's death, he remarked:

> Oh, considerably ... We had groups that we'd go out with. And I came back [from up north] and I said, 'I don't know how long it would be before they kicked me out.' It didn't take very long, so I sort of resented it.

Marcel had a different issue with invitations. He, like a couple of others, noted that he had received a lot of attention from neighbours and friends right after his wife died, but the attention had dissipated. He stated that when he coincidentally ran into neighbours outside their homes, they would invite him in for a drink or a beer right then and there. He would say that he already had plans because these same people never called him or made advance appointments. Some widowers thought that the disappearance of invitations might also have been a reflection of the friends' having been more attached to wives rather than to the men, themselves.

But They Were Really Her Friends

Eight men felt that the people they had trouble maintaining relationships with had primarily been their wives' friends.[1] When I asked Keith how his relationships with his friends had changed, he replied:

> Well, I don't think it's changed any. Well, like some of the people we associated with were Janet's friends ... [more] than my friends. So I don't see them that often. Just when I'm out shopping.

Leonard explained that he and his wife's friends had tried to continue the relationship, but:

> We had friends as a couple, and those friends it was very awkward around ... 'cause [they] were some friends that Carole was much closer to ... We tried to get together, but it was really just awkward ... just like trying to pretend ... But ... we never had a good friendship ... and so some of those friendships I didn't keep up, and they didn't keep up.

Stan also noted that there were friends whose attachment was really to his wife. He, unlike Leonard, was disappointed:

I hardly hear from them now. You don't even get a Christmas card ... it would be nice.

Stan's use of the word 'even,' underlines his feeling that a Christmas card symbolized the minimum amount of attention one might expect from people even if the relationship had been primarily with his wife. He commented that not hearing from his wife's friends was 'sudden.'

In contrast, Mel tried to keep up with friends in a nearby town who used to visit back and forth with him and his wife. He reflected:

Because my wife really made it a point to be with them a lot ... I've dropped by [their house] when I'm in the area. And they're not home so I leave them a note. And call, but there doesn't seem to be any contact ... I feel kind of bad about that. But I came to the conclusion that it was my wife ... that they were really friendly with. And because I was her husband, I was included. And I always felt very close to them. So, I feel bad about that. But maybe their circumstances have changed, too ... So there may be other reasons.

Mel was disappointed that this couple had not kept in touch with him even though he, unlike many widowers, had made several attempts to reach out to them.

Although these widowers interpreted the loss of their friendships through the belief that the individuals involved were really just friends with their wives, Helena Lopata (1996: 159-60) suggests some other possibilities. Although her work focused primarily on widows, these suggestions may apply to men as well. First, some people avoid 'all connections with death,' and, therefore, avoid spending social time with people who have been touched by it. Second, some people find interactions with widowed people 'awkward,' particularly if they were used to seeing the person as half of a couple. As well, the 'norms of symmetry and sharing' may no longer fit. Phrases such as 'third wheel' and 'odd man out' sum up how off balance these encounters may feel to both the friends who are still in couples and to the widowers themselves. Last, being widowed does confer lower status on men, and, therefore, upsets the equality of status that is a hallmark of friendship (Lopata, 1975; Allan, 1979; Suttles, 1970 cited in van den Hoonaard 2001: 69).

Other widowers stated they had never had many friends or that the changes in their friendships were a direct result of their having depended on their wives to keep up friendships and to arrange their social lives.

I Don't Have Close Friends

Eleven men pointed out, in one way or another, that they had not really had many friends even when they were married. They provided a variety of explanations related to their individual personalities, their situations, focusing their social relationships on their families, or their having depended on their wives to make social arrangements.

Three men said simply that they did not make friends. George, for example, said that he had few close friends because he had different interests from most people:

> I am not very much interested in some of the concerns, some of the interests of most people that I interact with. I'm an idea person. If I cannot discuss ideas ... share them with other people and have other people actually tear my ideas apart, That to me is very important. I'm not much interested in small talk.

This explanation served to stress George's academic achievements on which he relied, along with a scientific attitude, to claim these fragments of masculinity. Leroy, using the attribute of autonomy, observed that he had only superficial friends because, 'I'm not one to bare my soul too much to people.' Jacob's wife had been outgoing and gregarious, but he only had a few lifelong friends. He remarked that his wife had 100 friends and acquaintances for every one that he had.

Two widowers had few friends because of their circumstances rather than personality or preference. Matthew had done shift work during his working years and observed that it is difficult to make friends when you are a shift worker. Patrick's wife had had a long-term illness, and he explained that the contingencies of her health had diminished any opportunity to make friends.

Other widowers explained that, characteristic of many people in the Atlantic Provinces of Canada (Trovato & Halli 1983), their social lives had revolved around their families and their wives. Combine this social context with the tendency for men to rely on their wives for friendship, and we have a situation in which many men simply explained that they neither had nor needed friends. Stan, for example, after noting the loss of friendship with a particular couple, pointed out that his relationship with his family is his main concern:

> As long as I got immediate family, that's all that matters to me. I'm quite happy ... We never went out, or very rarely, as couples. It was more with the family unit. Like [my wife's] cousin and his wife ... But not like with out-of-family people ... But I don't miss people because I never had them to miss.

Grant and his wife's social life revolved around their family, but he made an even stronger point that he and his wife had been all the friends they needed:

> But we were so close to one another, we didn't need anybody else. I guess that was the truth of it ... Perhaps we should have been more cognizant of our friends' needs ... But we were quite content with one another's company.

Similarly Charles explained:

> But we always, our whole lifetime, we did a lot of things together. Not with other people. In other words, we never mind[ed] going on vacation together or out to dinner together. We didn't always have to be with somebody else.

For Charles, his and his wife's enjoyment in one another's company was an indicator of a strong relationship. He continued:

> And I always, I noticed lately ... I see older couples eating breakfast [in a restaurant], having no conversation, whatsoever. Now I don't know if they're married or just friends. But I can't understand with my wife that there would be just no conversation.

Charles and his wife clearly never ran out of things to say to one another. Both Charles and Grant had a small or nonexistent friendship network, and they perceived their situation as evidence of the strength of their marriage. Neither seemed to regret his exclusive focus on his wife as his only close friend.

Florida widowers Samuel and Bernie indicated that they had depended on their wives to make social arrangements. Samuel, who explicitly pointed out that he had no interest in making friends with men said:

[How would you say that your life changed since Hannah died?] Well, my life changed because she used to take care of all the social arrangements. I really didn't have that much to do with it. Also she would make many lady friends whereas I would not make any men friends ... the ability to make friends was really a female ... something that ladies were better at than I was. So she would make a lot of lady friends. And then, after she died, I suddenly had no friends. (Samuel)

Bernie described a similar situation in which he simply relied on his wife and had never had to make his own friends. His sense of feeling lost was palpable when he commented that:

I thought I would never have another friend.

Fortunately, for Bernie, people with whom he had become friends through his wife continued to stop by to visit.

Seven participants, all but one of whom were older than 75 at the time of our interview, talked about losing most of their friends through illness and death. As others have found, these men did not form new friendships that would replace those who died (Fischer and Oliker 1983, cited in Wright 1988: 214). These included former colleagues (Ralph), family (Stan), and people with whom he had moved to Florida (Izzy). Tim, who was 79, spoke at length:

I still got most of the friends I had before – ones that are living. Like this street here. I used to know everybody on this street. Now there's only about four or five of the older families that I remember that are still here ... That's what I miss. You talk about friends, that's what I miss most of anything are friends that have died. They have died or they don't get out or are in nursing homes or something like that. So, I don't, as a rule, make any new friends, but I lost a lot of old ones.

Tim's comment that his neighbourhood had changed is significant because neighbours were very important to some of the men. The next section will look at what the men said about their neighbours.

Relationships with Neighbours

Although there may have been some neighbours who were also friends, the men made a definite distinction between neighbours and friends.

Several found that neighbours were particularly supportive right after their wives' deaths. Two men commented on the decline of neighbouring in their experience while two others pointed out that the friendliness and helpfulness of neighbours is characteristic of small towns.

Leroy lives in a small town that is primarily an area for summer cottages. Thus, when winter comes, there is only a small nucleus of about ten families that remain. He recounted that:

> I had a lot of support [at the time my wife died] ... We were pretty close and people knew that ... So I had quite a bit of sympathy ... a lot of support from local neighbours ... I used to have to chase them away because they were bringing so much food.

Leroy described the reciprocal practice that the people who stayed in the winter had of checking up on one another. He was quite explicit, however that this pattern was a 'semi-duty' that was more related to neighbourliness than friendship. The practice of mutual assistance is entrenched in Atlantic Canada. The harsh Canadian winter combined with the rural environment results in strong norms of mutual helping among neighbours.

The men who lived in small towns made particular comments about what the community and neighbours have meant to them. Winston and Bob both felt a part of their semi-rural towns and commented on the friendliness of those small towns. Their local identities served them well. Matthew, on the other hand, felt his outsider status in his community keenly after his wife died. He was no longer included in social events such as sleigh rides.

Ralph had been a part of his village for a long time, but he had observed changing patterns of neighbouring. He bemoaned the change:

> So, back on the social end of things. Well, for years, nobody – ever since TV came along. Nobody visits their neighbours any more anyway. That's a fact. So there's no visiting neighbours.

Patrick also had less contact with neighbours. In his case, the neighbourhood had changed around him, and university students had replaced age peers:

> But, in this neighbourhood, you don't get too friendly with your neighbours ... See you have a student house across [the street], and you have a

student house down below. And three houses up here, you've got student houses all over the street.

Both Patrick and the students related to each other solely in terms of their divergent ages. Patrick's sense of comfort as a long-time inhabitant of his neighbourhood where he had a known identity as a resident (Matthews 1979) had departed along with his former neighbours. For the students who live on his street, Patrick's most salient characteristic, his master status (Hughes [1945] 1984), is his age and vice versa.

The material above might give one the impression that all of these men lived isolated lives with only brief, superficial contact with people who lived near them. This notion is incomplete. The next section discusses what the men said about friendships that did continue.

Continuing Friendships

The men described a variety of styles of friendship. Keith and Marc, neither of whom was retired, spoke about friends from their work. Keith's work friends lived 25 miles away. Marc compared his experience with his colleagues to his being dropped from invitation lists for events that included couples. In contrast, he noted that lists for work-related events:

> included my own co-professionals and co-workers ... it was quite an extended group ... There was no problem there because we performed some activities without our spouses annually ... there was no exclusion because there was no danger.

Although Marc's colleagues may have been married, marital status was not an issue in these activities because everyone participated in them as an individual rather than as a member of a couple. Neither of these men had retired at the time of the interview. It is impossible to predict whether or not they will be able to maintain these connections once they leave the workplace.

Just as for Marc, others alluded to groups either comprised entirely of men or that included both single men and women which they found very supportive. For example, Matthew referred to a group of men who met at a local restaurant for coffee every morning. Herbert and Marcel each went out for meals with mixed groups that were not based on couples. There is no indication that the members of these groups met socially outside the group context. Shared knowledge provided the members of these groups with a common basis that reinforced their sense of belonging (Kaplan 2006) and localness which bolstered their masculinity.

The most striking description of friendship came from Ed, a widower in the Florida group. Ed provided a lengthy and detailed description of how his friendships functioned. The components of this summary highlight the extent of the difference between Ed's and the other men's experiences. It also sheds light on the social context of retirement communities, for the way in which his friendships functioned required the activities which are emblematic of retirement-community living.

I Have a Wonderful Bunch of Friends Here

There are three themes that stand out in Ed's discussion of his relationship with his friends: support, invitations, and reciprocity. As well, Ed compared his experience favourably with that which he believed is more typical.[2] Ed underlined his belief that he was an exception by bringing up the special nature of his friendships in response to questions dealing with a variety of topics ranging from how his life had changed to whether or not he thought he would remarry. Very early in the interview, as part of his response to my general question about his experience with losing his wife, Ed described how his wife had died and then remarked:

> What can I tell you after that? I have a very good support group here, an excellent support group.

Ed's doctor had suggested an organized support group, but Ed found that, not only was he not interested in telling his problems to strangers or hearing theirs, but:

> My friends, here, believe me, are wonderful. And they were our friends, and they didn't drop me once Ruth passed away.

Immediately, Ed made it clear that I might be incredulous, 'believe me,' and that being dropped by friends when widowed is a common occurrence (van den Hoonaard 1994). Ed's friends were willing to talk to him while he was grieving and continued to talk about Ruth in their conversations.

Not only had Ed not been dropped by his friends, but they also included Ed when they went out for dinner, a centrepiece of Florida retirement-community social life, as well as to the theatre and on short vacations. He explained:

> If they do anything or go anywhere, 'Ed, you're coming.' Not, 'do you want to?' But I go ... And like I say, they go somewhere, 'Ed, you're coming.' We go see a show someplace, 'I'm getting you a ticket.' 'Fine, get me a ticket.' And so instead of getting two, they get one [for me], and I'm grateful for them.

As with other accounts of widowhood in a retirement community (van den Hoonaard 1994), this description includes the couples' doing the inviting, deciding where to go, and the widower's feeling gratitude for the invitation. These ingredients in Ed's relationship suggest that he occupied a lower status than his married friends who made all the decisions, but for Ed, this situation was far better than most widowed people encountered in retirement communities.

Ed's story also includes reciprocity, an element that is absent from virtually every other widower's discussion of relationship with friends. Although it was clearly his couple friends who took the initiative to include him in their plans and invite him to dinner, Ed remarked:

> And I mean, I'll reciprocate. I won't cook, but I'll say, 'Come on up for drinks. And then we'll go out to eat.'... You know, you don't take constantly. You've got to give occasionally, and it works both ways.

Finally, interspersed throughout Ed's description of his good experience with his friends are comments that compare his experience with those of other widowed people and his own disappointment with friends from up north:

> I don't feel like a fifth wheel ... And I tell [others] of my friends here, and they're amazed that they stand by me ... My friends ... are a little disappointment up north ... my friends down here are much better than the ones up north.

Ed provided a cautionary tale of what can happen if your friends are not loyal:

I have one gal ... Her husband passed away, and ... after two or three
weeks, all of her friends, married friends deserted her ... And she ... mar-
vels at the relationship that we have in our condo.

Many of the men discussed the minor place their friends had in their
lives and said they had no one to confide in. Ed, however, used terms
like my 'mainstay' and 'key' to characterize the significance of his unusual relationship with his friends. His social life had barely changed,
and he exclaimed that, because of the friendship and support of his
social group, he did not see any reason to consider remarriage. He
summed up his opinion by saying:

That's why I say I'm very grateful for the friends ... and they're my support group. I don't need anything else or anybody else.

The men's discussions of their friendships, many of which were lost
in widowhood, bring to mind the work of Sarah H. Matthews (1986) on
friendship styles in old age. Matthews identified three styles or ways of
doing friendship: independent, discerning, and acquisitive. The 'in-
dependents' were not isolated but rather saw themselves as self-sufficient. Like George, Leroy, and Stephen, they made a point of saying that
they did not make strong connections with friends and would not bare
their souls to anyone. Similarly, Stratton and Moore (2003: 19) comment
that none of the Jewish widowers in their study had a close friendship
with a non-related man.

Discerning styles of friendship result in one's having very specific
standards for someone to be called a friend, often related to the length
of the friendship. Jacob might fit this category. As well, the men who
did not have any friends left because they had died would fit here.
They did not consider the possibility of acquiring new friends so late
in life. The men who made a distinction between neighbours and
friends or between acquaintances and friends are also discerning.
Neighbours were very important, but they did not meet the high standards of friendship.

People with acquisitive friendship styles continue to form new
friendships wherever they go and in whatever situation they find themselves. Perhaps the only person who was this open to friendship was
Ed, who grabbed on to what was offered by a very supportive group of
people and expressed his gratitude for them whenever possible.

Sarah Matthews does not include an explicit gender analysis in her discussion, although the examples she uses to illustrate the independent friendship style are primarily men. She does, however, point out that when 'turnings' occur that catapult someone into a new stage of life (Mandelbaum, cited in Matthews 1986), for example a change in marital status, those with an acquisitive style are most likely to react using the change as an opportunity to make new friends.

We are left with the stories many widowers told of friendships that seemed to wither away naturally. They had lost their foundation either because the friends had, indeed, been attached more to the men's wives or because the 'odd-man-out' and 'fifth-wheel' feeling could not be overcome. These men had had married lives that were 'couple oriented,' and they were now excluded from or uncomfortable in 'couple gatherings' (Matthews 1986: 109). They were identifying their discomfort at being single men in a 'couples' world' (van den Hoonaard 2001).

Jerome Tignoli (1980) suggests that homophobia, competitiveness, and inexpressiveness are components of masculinity that inhibit man-to-man friendships. It may also be that our seeing women as specialists in friendship (Davidson, Daly and Arber 2003) means that we do not always recognize what men are telling us. Bleiszner and de Vries (2000: 130) point out that men are likely to provide 'proxy indicators' such as frequency of contact and length of acquaintance to communicate the strength of friendship, while women highlight the emotional components of their friendships.

For many of the widowers, being active and having 'friendly relations' (Kurth 1979 cited in Matthews 2000: 158) with people were more significant than having close friends. Their shared activities provided a sense of solidarity and homogeneity (Adams et al. 2000), which also serve as proxy indicators of friendship, particularly in Atlantic Canada. The activities might, as Kaplan has argued (2006:591), have served as a 'displacement' or 'containment' of the widowers' emotions by providing homosocial events where they could share similar interests and demonstrate masculine competence. These friendly relations depended on the men's being active in social settings outside their homes, and the next chapter explores how the widowers talked about their activities and everyday lives.

PART FOUR

Experiencing Everyday Life

8 Everyday Life in and out of the House

The absence of their wives as companions in their activities was a frequent theme in the lives of older widowers, although the approaches and levels of participation varied. Being busy is a notable antidote for loneliness, and the widowers located the responsibility for finding things to do in themselves. For many, being alone and being lonely were virtually synonymous. A few other men had worked at solitary jobs throughout their lives, and, therefore, did not find being alone as challenging.

To avoid a solitary existence, the men needed to avoid spending too much time in their houses. The feeling of being in the house alone was very difficult for some men. The widowers associated staying home throughout the day with loneliness and ruminating on their loss. For some, their wives' deaths afforded them the opportunity to spend more time with outside activities and the freedom to come and go as they pleased.

Some men found the opportunity to get out of the house through participating in formal, organized activities. Most avoided seniors' organizations and favoured organized activities that involved low levels of commitment. Their degree of involvement in volunteer activities and churches or synagogues varied.

The common thread to the men's discussions is a focus on keeping busy. The widowers saw being busy as a way to cope with loneliness, saw it as their responsibility, and felt that anybody could keep busy.

The Meaning of Being Alone

Being a widower meant doing things alone or being alone to a much greater extent than in the past, and loneliness and aloneness were the biggest challenge some men faced as widowers. In fact, the participants often did not distinguish between being alone and being lonely – these two concepts were virtually synonymous in their experience. When I asked Leroy what it was like to live alone, for example, he said:

Lonesome, that's all. Other than that, I get along fine.

Marcel focused on the solitariness of being in the house during the cold months:

I like to be alone ... but ... being alone at home in the winter, day by day without talking to anybody. It will drive you crazy.

Matthew moved to a larger centre because he felt ostracized in the small town he had lived in with his wife, but from which he had not come. He described his situation as:

And then I never saw anybody for six, seven months. Just isolated up there in this big, old house. So I moved [to the city].

The men also noted that they were now doing many things alone, for example, going to lectures and travelling. Most significant were those activities they would have previously done with their wives. Tim remarked that his life had not changed very much but:

I just keep doing the same things pretty well that I was doing before, only I'm doing them alone now.

George said that travelling was something he preferred to do with company:

I'd like to be with someone ... I really don't like travelling alone ... somehow it's much more meaningful to be able to sound [out] what you're saying [because someone reacts to your ideas].

In fact, George often took trips with his sister-in-law.[1] Herbert used to go to hockey games with his wife. Now, 'I've got to hunt up somebody or go alone.'

Charles found that the feeling of activities he had previously done alone had changed. In the past, when he was going out alone, the knowledge that his wife would be there when he returned home resulted in his not being lonely:

> [My wife played cards on Friday night, and it was] my movie night. I would go alone. And I didn't mind going alone. But now I mind going alone. It's not the same. When I went to the movies [on] Friday night alone, she was home ... It was different.

As Kate Davidson (2004) has pointed out, men are interested in remarriage, at least partially, because they want someone to come home to. With no one to come home to, Charles has stopped going to the movies on Friday nights.

Herbert provided a particularly explicit example that characterizes being alone and loneliness as permeating his life:

> And this is the biggest thing, being alone. Loneliness is the worst thing. Being alone, doing everything alone. You don't have anybody to talk to. Maybe we talked more than most people, but we used to spend a lot of time just the two of us, sitting and talking.

In contrast, Stan 'missed [his] wife terribly,' but he had already been used to spending time alone because of his working conditions. He commented that his life had not changed very much since his wife's death. He explained:

> It's lonely, but my job was lonely. So I kind of was accustomed to it ... Unless you're training somebody, you worked alone ... There's well, really, not that much difference for me where I was so accustomed to working alone.

Charles, who lives in a retirement community in Florida, had the opposite point of view. He suggested that for men, 'it's a different life,' with more changes than in women's lives when they become widowed. There are many widows in Florida, and married and single women socialize together.[2] Similarly, Izzy pointed out that when it comes to going out to restaurants in groups:

> Women can do it; men can't. I don't care what restaurant you go to down here, you'll always see a group of two, four, six women together. You never see two men, or four men, or six men.

Izzy suggested that if men went out to dinner together, people might assume they were homosexual.

The Atlantic Canadian context is quite different. It is very common to see groups of older men having coffee together at Tim Horton's, particularly in the morning. These men tend to arrive one by one and meet up with each other at the coffee shop rather than come together.

One way to guard against being alone and lonely for men is to get out of their houses and participate in a variety of activities. The next section looks at what men said about how they felt in their houses as widowers and the necessity to avoid spending too much time there.

Getting Out of the Widower's House

When participants' wives died, the meaning of being at home changed. This shift became evident through the way they talked about being alone in the house. Particularly in the early days of widowhood, most of the men equated spending a lot of time in the house with giving in to their grief. Finally, for both Canadian and Florida widowers, getting out of the house, as well as being active and seeing others, was an important avenue for coping with their loss.

Several men talked about the difficulties they had with being in their homes without their wives. Kate Davidson (1999: 112) has observed that many men are not used to being alone in their houses and may find the 'private isolation' of being in the house alone 'intolerable,' and these men's comments support her observation. Samuel, for example, found that his empty house shocked him with the loss of his wife:

> The evenings were very sad ... it was just like a bombshell, remembering Hannah, with the empty house.

Grant worked every day from nine to five at what was supposed to be a 'part-time job' that his Member of Parliament had given him 'out of kindness' to avoid being in his house alone.

Ralph told of the feeling of emptiness every time he opened the door:

> From a home point of view, for the first few months after her death, and particularly the first time I opened this door, I looked to see if she was playing Solitaire at the table ... and she wasn't there. And so the house was like a big, empty cavern, canyon, cave, anything you want to express it. There was an emptiness there, and I was looking for her and I couldn't

find her. And then gradually I accepted the fact ... I got this storey-and-a-half house all to myself, and I've got to live with it.

Just as Ralph communicates the hollowness of his house in a way that evokes a sense of being underground, Leonard describes a claustrophobic feeling as if his house had been 'closing in on me.'

As Leonard began to feel more comfortable in his house, he made the decision to stay at home on days when he needed to give free rein to his grieving:

Every now and then, I needed just to take a day off work, and I did. And stayed home. I'd write in my journal and cry ... Although it kind of meant that some days I would just stay home, it was better in the end for me.

For Leonard and Ed, staying home and grieving were clearly an occasional and conscious giving in to their situation. Neither of them suggested that he would make it a way of life. In fact, five of the Canadian widowers equated not getting out of the house with wallowing in misery. They conceptualized being at home too much as 'just sitting around':

I'm not just *sitting around* the house, moping. (Stan)

It's better to be busy than *sitting around* doing nothing, *sitting around* and thinking. (Herbert)

Now I don't *sit around*, kind of, 'what am I going to do with myself?' (Angus) [emphasis added]

Angus, in his explanation of how he ended up going to dances on weekends, described the alternative as:

I just didn't want *to sit* home, you know what I mean. [emphasis added]

The worst thing a widower can do is:

Just come in here and sit down or lay down on the couch and give up. (Bob)

The use by so many men of the phrase, 'sitting around,' suggests a shared, normative understanding of the meaninglessness of staying home, particularly during the day. Clearly, staying home all the time symbolizes giving up. Only a few referred to reading or watching television as viable activities. The men gave no indication that spending time doing housework or making repairs to their homes was a meaningful alternative to just sitting around when they were at home.

Spending a lot of time out of the house is one of the major ways that widowers avoid going 'stark, raving crazy' (Stan). Several men pointed out that getting out of the house was the way they dealt with loneliness and grieving:

> [Were there any times that were more difficult than others?] [When] you've got nothing to do ... Like an old dog, you go out [to] the road and look up and down the road, say, 'Which way am I going to go today?' ... Like I say, you just have to pick up and go somewhere ... Just get in the truck, head for town. (Bob)

> I go out as frequently as I can ... So what I do is go out–get the hell out of the house. (Jacob)

Patrick noted that he had been quite deliberate in his decision not to allow himself to 'fade away' the same way some of his acquaintances had after retirement. He remarked:

> I'll keep myself involved in community affairs ... whatever happens I'm going to keep myself involved ... I was going to keep myself involved so I wouldn't start feeling sorry for myself.

The repetition of the phrase, 'keep myself involved,' emphasized the importance it has for Patrick as well as the level of agency involved in his statement and the difference between him and men who were not successful in dealing with life transitions. Patrick did not wait for others to invite him out; he took the initiative.

Grant's comments highlight the loneliness of being at home with the recognition that, if he wanted to be around people, he would have to leave the house:

> I rattle around this house like a pea in a box. I get out quite a lot. Try to mix and socialize.

Grant's comment illustrates not only the loneliness of being at home but also the solitariness of being in the house. As others have found, few men had ever invited anyone into their house once their wives had died (Arber et al. 2003). Therefore, if they wanted to see another person, they had to leave the house:

> We never have any company ... In fact, you're the first company we've had because, well I'm out, you know ... as far as socializing, I do it outside. (Angus)

As Chad remarked:

> I like to have people around. I hate being alone. That's why I'm gone all the time, and I'm not home.

These comments about what it feels like in the house underline the feelings of warmth and home-ness that their houses lost when the participants' wives died. Images of the house as a cave, a box that is closing in, make these men's houses seem impersonal and cold. There seem to be very few, if any, activities for the men to do at home that are meaningful or interesting. It is not surprising that they would flee their houses as often as possible.

For the men whose wives had had a chronic illness, being a widower meant that they now had the 'freedom' to go out and socialize or be active. For example:

> I'm not around the house as much, like I used to be around here all the time with her, looking after her. 'Cause in the latter stages, even though ... she didn't look sick, she always had a life of crippling effect from [her illness]. (Stan)

Even Keith, whose wife did not have an illness that kept him around the house, found being a widower freeing:

> It's a lonely life at times, but I'm enjoying my independence, too. You know, I can come and go as I please.

In contrast, Leroy, himself, had a progressive, debilitating disease. He found that he was spending more time at home than he had when his wife had been with him. It was not only more difficult to get out physically, but he missed the spontaneity of their car trips:

> But now, since she's gone ... [I] don't jump in the car. And driving by myself, you know, what the heck for? So that's the biggest change, I would

say ... I'm more of a home-sticking, home person ... I haven't got a partner to go with.

Leroy identified his decline in activity as the most difficult aspect of his life since his wife died:

> I'm sticking home a lot more than we used to. Our lifestyle, my lifestyle has changed in that respect ... I'm not as mobile as I used to be ... I always was active. And I was always *out around* ... but I can't do this much, you see. [emphasis added]

There were only a few men who did not feel an imperative to be out of the house. They reported enjoying reading, watching television and cooking. Leonard, who had found himself so uncomfortable in his house at first, for example, noted that as time went on he:

> kind of got used to it and then ... began to enjoy my time alone ... So actually, I began to do things that I really enjoyed around the house ... baking bread and things like that. So, after awhile, actually, I liked it.

Leonard's enjoyment in being at home alone was an exception.

These men's attitudes about being in their house and the need to be out of the house much of the day reinforce findings by Cherry Russell (2007) that both women and men see the home as a 'woman's place' and 'women have been more involved in the domestic and emotional work of 'making' a home' (179). Getting out allows the men to escape the 'feminine space' (Meadows & Davidson (2006) that their houses represent.

Getting Out

The men used various strategies to be around people. Most frequently they described seemingly informal and unplanned mechanisms for socializing. A few men simply had to leave the house, and they could count on running into people whom they know. Stan, for example, explained that before he took up volunteering, he would merely take a walk in his neighbourhood and:

> Oh, you meet them around and enough, and the people there ... We knew each other anyway. And you'd say, 'Hello,' and some of them I used to know from [when I worked at] the station.

Leroy who lives in a more rural setting remarked that all he needed to do was sit on his porch and:

> I have quite a few neighbours come up and shoot the guff on the porch.

For Chad, the shopping mall provided an opportunity to socialize, particularly during inclement weather. Bob lived in a smaller town and said the he often went into the local store where he would:

> Talk to some of the boys in there. Or go do something else, or run into somebody in there that you knew.

He opined that this strategy would work in any small town. He compared the smaller community with a city where he believed, 'you wouldn't even know the neighbours that lived across the hall.' These Atlantic Canadians were truly locals, and they assumed that anyone in the town would have the same experience. It did not occur to them that men from away might not be so successful in finding people to 'run into.'

Marcel, who had immigrated from Southern Europe and lived in a small city, was still an outsider. In addition, he had been used to a café culture before coming to Canada. He explained:

> It's one of the things good about my country. You go out in the street, yourself. You meet people, say, 'Hey, how are you doing? Let's go for a coffee and talk about something ...' The people *talk* and you can be depressed but this is alleviated. You go home and [this] big break ... is very important. [emphasis in original]

Marcel said that he could still meet somebody on the street and say hello, but the person would usually turn down a suggestion to go for a coffee. As well, he found that Canadian men were more comfortable discussing hockey and other sports than personal issues.

Ironically, Marcel was missing an urban social context while the locals believed that people would not know each other in a city. The sense of belonging is not intrinsic to either rural areas *or* cities. Rather social integration provides the occasions for the informal, spontaneous sociability the men valued.

In the Florida retirement-community setting, the clubhouse and pool serve as central gathering places where one can go to 'run into' friends and acquaintances:

> Like I say, the pool is a meeting place. You meet everybody there eventu-
> ally. So if I want to be, you know, want people, I go down to the pool in the
> morning. If I want to be left alone, I just stay away. (Ed)

Ed did not mention that particular social groups have regular meeting times at the pool in a retirement community (van den Hoonaard
1992). When Ed talked about meeting 'everybody,' he was talking
about the social circle to which he belonged rather than all the residents of the community.

Widowers in Atlantic Canada also met up with friends who could be
counted on to frequent a particular social setting or event. Patrick provides a very creative approach. He described a full social life, much of
which was premised on his knowing where he would 'run into' acquaintances and friends:

> I go to quite a few concerts and things like that. Meet friends there. [What
> about weekends? Some people find weekends a little long.] No, I keep
> myself busy ... Everybody asks me where the church suppers are for the
> weekend. So ... I start looking about Wednesday for church suppers within
> about [a 30-mile radius]. And I'll go to a church supper on Saturday or a
> Sunday ... And you meet a lot of friends there, surprisingly enough. I see a
> lot of the same faces. So it almost got to the point where people got to the
> supper and say, 'Oh, I wonder if Patrick will be here ...'

Patrick described meeting up with his friends at events as 'surprising,' but it is also obvious that he knew very well that he would see
friends. He talked about 'running into' people at hockey games and
even remarked that he would often encounter friends at local restaurants who would invite him to join them for supper. His participation
in varied events and social settings is clearly strategic and depends on
his local credentials. The striking contrast with Marcel demonstrates
the significance of the outsider status of someone who 'came from
away' even though he has lived in Atlantic Canada for many years.[3]

Several men made a point of emphasizing that they were 'outdoors'
kind of guys whose activities evoked the traditional, Atlantic Canadian
way of life and were distinctly masculine. Keith and Bob talked about
hunting, fishing, and skiing alone, but they sometimes called friends
to arrange an outing on the spur of the moment. For example, Grant
cross-country skis in the winter and kayaks in the warmer weather.
He noted:

> We usually call one another up and 'meet you on the river,' or something
> like that. Usually ski up and down the river and go across the road here.
> Don't have to drive anywhere. Just put my skis on and go.

Bob explained that he would either call friends to meet for snowmobil-
ing or simply count on running into people. These examples of 'homosocial interaction' allow the men to 'maintain hegemonic masculine
norms' by reinforcing the identities they had as outdoors kinds of guys
whose personal identity conforms to 'hegemonic ideals' (Bird 1996:
124). As well, these men had known each other for many years. These
long-term friends, because they had known the widowers for a very
long time, contributed to the men's ability to maintain the personal
identities they preferred as real men rather than the social identity of
'widower' that came with the deaths of their wives (Siebert, Mutran, &
Reitzes 1999).

Jacob and Herbert each identified a 'current woman' (Moore and
Stratton 2002) with whom he got out of the house on a spontaneous
basis. Herbert talked about calling his sister-in-law on the spur of the
moment to go for an extended ride around the province or to try out a
new restaurant. Jacob called a woman friend, a 'buddy,' to go golfing.
These stories characterize the events as being arranged with a last-
minute phone call. They do not seem to entail any advance planning.
This lack of planning provides the spontaneity that many men miss
when their wives die.

Several men in Atlantic Canada performed odd jobs in their neighbourhood as a way of increasing their social contacts. Their discussions
emphasized localness and prototypical, male-typed practices. These activities emphasize masculine skills at the same time they enable the
men to avoid being alone. Bob, for example, helped his neighbours skin
and cut up moose during the short hunting season. He explained that
these odd jobs 'kept your mind away from [thinking about your loss]'
while Chad explained:

> I like to have people around. I hate being alone ... So, this afternoon, if it
> doesn't rain, I'm going across the street ... to put water repellent on [my
> neighbour's] deck ... I just do odds and ends like that. I built a deck for a
> guy this spring ... keeps you busy.

The unplanned and spontaneous feel one gets from the participants'
descriptions of their strategies for getting out of the house and doing

things with people is striking. They have incorporated a minimum of commitment and a strong sense of being free to 'come and go as I please' with which the men characterized their lives as widowers. These widowers fit into the category of 'company seekers' that Galit Nimrod and Hanna Adoni (2006) have identified as one of the clusters in their analysis of leisure-styles of recent retirees.[4] The characteristics of this group, members of which are disproportionately male, include 'a high frequency of meeting friends, freeform activities, and independent home activities' (2006: 617).

A few men described participating in groups that straddle the informal-formal dichotomy. Izzy, for example, played cards with a regular gaming group (van den Hoonaard 1992) at the clubhouse in his retirement community a few nights a week while both Samuel and Chad attended weekend breakfast clubs. Some of the widowers did participate in formal organizations and/or do regular volunteer work. The next section looks at how the men discussed their involvement in these groups.

Participation in Formal Groups

Most of the men did not participate extensively in formal organizations. There were a number who had been active in the past, and five who described being involved in ways that required very little commitment or regular activity. Two men explicitly stated that they were not 'joiners,' while two others described a level of participation in a variety of organizations that was quite broad. It was not unusual for the men who talked about their connections with organizations to note that they had been active and/or officers of the organizations in the past.

Charles, for example, had been involved with organizations that revolved around activities with his children. He remarked: .

> When our kids were young, we weren't people who sent them to activities. We took them and we stayed and we took part – was leaders at Scouts and Beavers. We've been in Lion's Club, and Jaycees, and [my wife] was in Jaycettes. I did all that stuff ... and then I got tired of it, and I quit.

Ralph had also scaled down his involvement as he got older, but he articulated this diminution more in terms of having done the work when he was the appropriate age and being content to hand it on to the next generation:

Well, socially, I'm not a joiner ... but a life member in the Squadron ... I've receded completely from the community. I had my day of helping out ... I've done the whole gamut, but younger people pick up the torch ... I can sit back now and say, 'Well, I was there.'

Bernie noted that he had had to be involved in organizations as part of his job when he was working and, therefore, was quite happy to relinquish his engagement when he retired.

Five men belonged to organizations that did not involve active participation or commitment. George, for example, kept up his memberships in scholarly organizations while Izzy maintained his membership in the Veterans Association whose meetings he no longer attended.

Bernie attended a computer club while Angus described a private club to which he belonged with some friends where:

Only men are allowed ... It was a Sergeant's Mess years ago, and they are very strict about membership ... I go in sometimes for half an hour, Friday night, maybe a Saturday afternoon for an hour. I don't stay. I don't go regular all the time ... It's nice to drop in and you have a drink ... and you chit chat ... go in and get the news. I don't think I belong to much else.

This kind of organization is typical of the traditional groups that are exclusively male and have a 'salience and sanctioned male bonding' that is an ideal of masculine friendship (Kaplan 2006: 572).

The lack of commitment involved in participating in these organizations is notable. The club or organization is there, and you can turn up whenever you feel like it. The widowers would agree with the Australian men (Russell 2007: 180) who did not like to be 'organized' or 'regimented' in their recreational pursuits. Rather they, 'preferr[ed] to 'do their own thing,' in their own time, and at their own pace.'

Matthew was one of the only men who attended a local seniors' centre, and he went with his girlfriend. This centre provides organized activities throughout the week including computer classes, a lecture series, social activities and fitness programs. He commented:

Janet and I both belong to [the centre] ... I've been to two or three Tai Chi classes where I'm the only male in the class of fifty women, and it's great. You get treated like a king.

Matthew had eschewed the seniors' activities in the small town from which he had moved several months after his wife's death. He described his experience of village life as being 'very lonely, kind of like a lost sheep,' and widowers go to the Seniors' Club and 'sit around and play bridge or some silly, little board game.' In the city, where he attended with his friend, he did not have the same difficulty. In fact, he was treated like a 'king,' a symbol of powerful male dominance. Cherry Russell (2007: 182) notes that men may shy away from participating in organizations geared towards older people because they do not include activities 'associated with traditional male interests such as sport ...' For Matthew, the small town, with its feminine activities, was an emasculating setting. In an urban centre he felt 'almost like being an elder bachelor all over again.' His story suggests that he had to leave the small town to once again be treated like a man, and his romantic connection with a woman made all the difference.

The preponderance of women is not unusual in organizations that cater to an older population (Davidson et al. 2003b). Herbert described the support group for widowed persons that he attended as made up predominantly of women. He explained that he had been invited to join the group by a woman friend whom he had known for a long time. He said:

> I started going last December ... I'd known [the widow] who invited me for 20 years. And I said, she wouldn't invite me to anything that wasn't right. I know her, I know the kind of person she is ... It's a very good group ... [we're] all going through the same thing.

Herbert might have preferred a men's group, but commented that there would not be enough widowed men in his area to form such a group.

Herbert's comment that he had decided to accept the invitation to join the group because he trusted his widow friend not to invite him to something that 'wasn't right' alerts us to the potential complications that can arise for widowers when they participate in organizations where there are single women in attendance. Mel withdrew from a square-dance club because he did not want to be tied down to a particular partner:

> I joined a square-dance group ... And really enjoyed it. And then there was one woman who was single again ... Prior to her arrival ... I was just

dancing with anybody that didn't have a partner at the time ... free lance. But she expected me to dance with her all the time ... It got so bad in my mind that I stopped going to the group.

It is hard to tell from Mel's description – and perhaps he did not know for sure – whether this woman would have pursued him outside of the club as well.[5] It is clear that Mel found having a regular partner too much obligation. He simply withdrew.

Researchers Lund and Caserta (2001: 162) report that many of the men who joined support groups for widowed persons explained that they had joined those groups with the possibility of meeting women in mind. Consistent with their comment, one mixed-gender, widowhood support group in Atlantic Canada had to cease functioning because the men were interested in seeking out couple relationships while the women were not.

Two men, Mel and Herbert, specifically mentioned that they had been invited to join 'seniors" groups but had declined. Mel, at 68, felt too young to be involved with seniors' groups. His comments reflect a general attitude that belonging to seniors' groups means hanging around with old people and most people, regardless of their age, do not perceive themselves to be old (Strain 2001):

> When my wife first passed away, I was asked to join the seniors' group at our church ... And I don't feel like a senior ... I thanked them for calling, but I don't attend. If I end up in a nursing home some day, I'll know I'm a senior. Put out to pasture.

Although Herbert, who was involved in a number of organizations, did not explicitly say so, he may have been avoiding 'seniors' organizations' because they are dominated by women and the activities may seem like the sorts of things that 'old women' enjoy doing – for example, playing cards or bingo (Davidson et al. 2003b).

In contrast, Patrick was heavily involved in organized activities ranging from his church to the Royal Canadian Legion, seniors' organizations, and organized bowling, curling, and golf. He noted that he had held leadership positions in these groups. Patrick saw this level of participation as the way to stay busy:

> I'm in quite a few organizations. So it keeps us, keeps me occupied ... These organizations keep me occupied.

In addition to more leisure- or social-related organizations, seven men were involved in volunteer work. They saw this kind of activity as a way to be of service, and also as a way to relieve loneliness, meet people, and keep busy. They also found volunteering to be enjoyable.

The two most common motivations for being volunteers, each identified by five men, were to help or be of service and that volunteering is pleasurable. Winston, for example, spent time volunteering in schools reading to Grade Two classes. He commented that:

> I think it's important that the world goes on the right way.

He had asked himself what he could do that might have a positive impact. Along with reading, Winston talked about the environment with the children. Winston had a history of doing volunteer work as a Rotarian both in the past and continuing at the time of our interview.

Al also talked about being of service but in a more informal way. He often drove other residents of his retirement community to doctors' appointments:

> I am also happy to be able to help my friends ... drive them around when they need help. Like We-Care[6] sort of approach. And I do that a lot.

Similarly, Bernie enjoyed helping his neighbours with driving, but he pointed out that he was not a 'volunteer, generally':

> I'll gladly help anybody out that needs a ride, but I don't want to be on anyone's list.[7]

This type of volunteering is particularly relevant in retirement communities in Florida, where many people live far away from their children and the 'ideological assumption' is 'we are all one' (Rubinstein 1986: 205, van den Hoonaard 1992).

Volunteering was also pleasurable. Chad, for example, belonged to the Men's Club at his church and enjoyed the work he did for that organization. He explained:

> I take part in the work ... put on dinners. And every spring we have a big ham, home-delivered ... dinner, and I work at that. I enjoy that stuff. And again, I guess I get to meet people.

Samuel played the piano at his synagogue. He commented that it kept him busy and that he used his playing to try to make dates with women at the synagogue.

The men's reasons for volunteering did not fit into simple, one-dimensional categories. Most identified more than one aspect of volunteering that was meaningful for them. Stan brought up his volunteering before I had asked a single question and referred to it in response to a variety of questions. He was particularly eloquent in this regard. He provided a detailed, multi-faceted discussion of his volunteering and the role it played in his life:

> It ... helped relieve me of my loneliness ... It's not my nature to go [to parties]. I like to help out ...with the police department ... Vial for Life ... I love it down at the office ... when the [tourist] ships come in, and they're waiting for tours of the brewery. I corner them ... and I get them to sign my [guest] book. And I'm on the police committee that meets once a month ... And you're helping the neighbourhood and the kids ... now they got me on full time ... at the police station.

Stan works five days a week as a volunteer and on weekends when the police have 'bike rodeos' at which they promote bicycle safety. Stan's description of his volunteering characterizes it as important, encompassing, and work-like. As well, his involvement alleviates the danger of both not having enough to do and of loneliness:

> It's been a big thing for me now. I might've got bored, and I did ... the loneliness ... You get so involved with the people ... it's taken the loneliness away. I *enjoy* it ... I just have fun ... And you're doing some good and usually, they do say thank you. So I think it's a godsend for me. [emphasis in original]

Stan suggested that while others might have visited patients in the hospital that's 'not [his] cup of tea.' Stan's style of volunteering encompasses the work-like aspect of volunteering with a masculine organization, the police, that men often describe.

There were two men who specifically pointed out that they did not and would not volunteer. George, who had worked with dyslexic youth earlier in his life, had thought about, but not taken any action, doing literacy work with ex-convicts. He had considered working for the local Alzheimer Society and recognized its importance, but observed, 'I don't have the patience for that.' Jacob, on the other hand, told me that people had suggested that he ought to volunteer, perhaps to assuage his loneliness, but:

> It's difficult for me to work for somebody else. I never did it successfully. After I became an adult male, I was always running the show. So I never could have adjusted back to work for you or anybody else. I can't do what I'm told [like volunteers do] ... I'm not good unless I'm the head honcho.

These two descriptions emphasize the speakers' preference for the male centre. When someone suggests that he had a very active life that emphasized his work as 'autonomous' and locates himself as the 'focus of attention,' he is taking the male centre in his answers (Aléx et al. 2008: 453-4). Jacob, in particular, characterized himself as the dominant male who could not do what he was told as a woman might.

Another area of activity for some widowers is their church or synagogue, and for a number of men it constituted an important component of their lives. The next section looks at how the widowers talked about their participation in and the meaning of church and synagogue activities in their lives.

Participation in Organized Religious Activities

The men reported a variety of levels of participation and meaningfulness of participation in religious activity. The level and type of support they received from their churches and synagogues were directly related to the nature of their involvement. As well, a number of the men reported that the amount of their participation in religious organizations and practice had changed since their wives' deaths.

Eight men explicitly stated that they took part in some organized religious activity on a regular basis. Seven went to churches and the eighth attended a synagogue. None of the widowers from Florida attended synagogue on a regular basis. Four of the men talked of a deep, Christian faith that led directly to a level of engagement in their churches that permeated the very fabric of their lives. They were not only active; they also held leadership positions. Grant explained that:

> The choir was the most important [activity] ... and I am still on various boards of the church. In particular the Worship Committee ... I was chairman of the board ... [I'm at the church] several times during the week.

This high level of involvement in the church has made a huge difference for Grant in his small town because he was from away. I asked him if he found himself treated as 'someone from away,' and therefore an outsider, once his wife had died. He agreed that he might have found himself in that position if he had not been active in his church. Grant did not have a pragmatic motive for participating in his church, but he knew that it had made a difference. Similarly, Mel suggested that:

> If we had arrived here and were new to the church, I don't think it would have been the same thing at all. And of course, my daughter and her family attend there. And maybe part of the reason that they were so friendly, too, is because of her.

In contrast, Leonard had begun to attend synagogue after the death of his wife and found his congregation very supportive.

Two of the widowers attended church every week but, for them, attendance was more out of habit than anything else. Neither stated that he had a deep faith or that his faith had been helpful to him in dealing with the loss of his wife. Bob, who is remarried, explained:

> We go to church. Always did. I went to church, and I went to church after ... when I was alone. Yes, we still go. My wife, now, we belong to the same church ... we always went. So, it was just a habit you went, just the same.

Winston included his description of church activity within his discussion of activities in general. It did not appear to play a special role in his life. The local church was simply one more local organization that he supported.

Seven men participated in their church or synagogue on a fairly sporadic basis. This was sometimes health related, as it was for Ralph who stated that he could no longer get up from kneeling for communion without help.

Three of the men who attended church on an occasional basis connected their attendance with being accompanied by a woman. Stan admitted that he was not involved in his church:

> Like I used to be. Very little, to be truthful ... It's sad to say. That could come back. If I became involved with somebody, it probably would ... It's not because of the deaths or anything; it's just the way I go. Every once in awhile, I'll get into the groove, and I'll start going like mad. So, it's my personality.

Stan's opinion that he might start going to church regularly if he developed a relationship with a woman is supported by Matthew and Angus who both said that they went to church with woman friends. Matthew who did not have a strong religious faith had twice gone to the church favoured by the woman with whom he was living. He remarked:

> I haven't really formed an opinion of that ... Religion never turned me on that much.

Only one widower from Florida, Al, described a regular association with a synagogue. He went on the High Holy Days (two or three days in the fall). Al also continued to pay dues and belonged to a synagogue up north so that the rabbi would, 'come and do my service [funeral] some day.'

Just as Stan reported a changed level of religious involvement on the death of his wife, several other widowers had also reduced their participation. Bernie and Jacob both explained that they had downplayed their atheism while their wives were alive. Bernie's comments indicated the normativeness of participation in religious rituals:

> And I've neglected to tell you, and I don't know why, because I still have this sense of secretiveness about this because it's not accepted generally ... But one of the liberating aspects of my widowhood was the fact that I no longer have to pretend ... I just felt that I was helping other people [by participating in Seders⁸ and other rituals]. I don't want to be disruptive, you know ... So, as I've said, it's free, it's liberating, and I can talk to you about it. And I wanted you to know it because I've been up front with you on everything else.

Leonard, Herbert, and Marcel had all increased their participation in religious activities since their wives' deaths. Leonard and his wife had led a secular life, and he said that the enormity of his wife's death really 'shook him' and he:

> look[ed] at the world differently ... [I read] some books on death and dying from [my religion's perspective] ... that was really helpful ... and gradually, I just read more and more and got involved in the synagogue locally.

Herbert found it easier to read the Bible and pray each morning because he no longer had anyone to take care of; Marcel, whose wife had been more religious than he, explained that he had been going to church more often because it helped maintain a close feeling with his wife.

The Importance of Keeping Busy

When you look at everything the men said about their activities, the common thread is being active and keeping busy. Many of the men explicitly stated that being occupied was both a way to cope with the loneliness and grieving of widowhood and an individual responsibility. Patrick, for example, commented that:

> I guess it's lonesome at times, but I keep myself occupied ... So that's been the principle ... The more you're involved ... It keeps me from going into the doldrums.

Similarly, Herbert explained:

> You've got to get up and go again. And I have been. I've been getting out and going ... The calendar this week looks almost full. It keeps me busy. It's better to be busy than sitting around, doing nothing. Sitting around and thinking.

The implicit message in Herbert's remarks that *you* have to get busy is that it is one's personal responsibility to find something to do. As Bob insisted:

> There's always something to do. Or [somewhere] to go. If you make up your mind to do it.

Similar to seeing staying at home as an indicator of not coping well with grief, the widowers saw failing to find things to do with one's time as leading to boredom and melancholy. Keeping busy is so important that Ed commented that it does not matter what you do. Anything is better than inactivity :

> You have to keep busy. Absolutely. You know, that's very important. Keeping busy and having people around you ... One thing I learned to do is keep myself busy, which is very important ... *So it's just anything. It doesn't really matter* ... I need to keep busy and keep occupied. [emphasis added]

Only two men admitted that they had trouble finding enough things to do, Bernie who had 'eventually' developed a routine, and Tim who said:

> I find that I have a lot of time on my hands, keep finding it harder to do any work now like I used to.

Contrast his comments with George who boasted:

> I'm one of those people – I have had such a diversity of interests that I'm never bored ... boredom has never been one of my problems.

In their everyday lives, the men saw no difference between 'being alone' and 'being lonely.' They disliked spending too much time in their houses and therefore valued activities that got them out of the house. At the same time, most widowers preferred activities that did not entail ongoing obligations. The exception to preferring the freedom of not being committed to a particular activity at a particular time is participation in one's church, although only a few men described deep involvement in their churches.

The focus on loneliness and the need to get out of the house in order to avoid giving up and sitting and dwelling on the past brings to mind John Bayley's book, *Widower's House*. Bayley saw his house, in his first days as a widower, as, 'a refuge rather than a home. A lair.' He suggests that he longed to return to his house when 'forced' to leave it. When Bayley did get home, he felt the house's 'emptiness' without his wife, Iris Murdoch (2001: 115), just as Robert Rakoff (1977) suggests that it is the activity of family life that makes a house into a home.

As Bayley recovered from his deep grief, he began to leave his house voluntarily and eventually left it entirely. *Widower's House* includes the symbols of loneliness, emptiness, and rumination that the participants in this study associated with spending their days alone in their houses. John Bayley had to leave his widower's house for good in order to live again, and most of the participants needed to leave their houses every day in order to find meaning in their lives.

Robert Rubinstein (1986) notes that going out during the day and coming home at the end of the day is particularly important for older men who live alone. He conceptualizes men's regular departure from their homes as 'getting out,' a phrase a number of widowers used. As well, Rubinstein points out that being out of the house is not just the physical departure but also an opportunity for social interaction. The social aspect of getting out is particularly important because most men do not invite friends into their homes to socialize.

As we have seen in this chapter, many men preferred getting out to be spontaneous, non-directed, and undemanding (Rubinstein 1986: 149). They often participated in what Ray Oldenburg, in *The Great Good Place*, (1989: 16) refers to as a 'third place':[9] 'A generic designation for a great variety of public places that host the regular, voluntary, informal, and happily anticipated gatherings of individuals beyond the realms of home and work.'

These venues, according to Oldenburg, provide neutral ground where one sees friends on a regular, but not obligatory, basis. One can count on seeing familiar faces in the third place, where the main activity is conversation. These hangouts are overwhelmingly male and include saloons, coffee counters, pool halls, and clubs. In rural areas, third places include hunting and fishing shacks. Oldenburg's tone is decidedly nostalgic, but the church suppers, clubs, hardware stores, snowmobile runs, and retirement-community swimming pools communicate the importance of a third place for those widowers who do not want obligations to structure their time but who do want social encounters as part of their everyday lives. As well, these third places give a man a sense of belonging to a collectivity that may contribute the 'possession of a higher self-worth,' which reinforces his 'image of himself in wider society' as a real man (Duneier 1992: 112).

The third places that the widowers described provide an opportunity for sociability rather than intimate conversation (Simmel 1950: 52). Sociability entails meetings where the sole purpose is sociable conversation in which the topic is simply the medium through which one can have a 'lively exchange,' the attraction of the event. The widowers, by engaging in sociability, can leave the house, get out to one of these social settings, and 'shoot the breeze' in order to escape the lonely, solitary places that their houses have become. Part of Marcel's disappointment with the conversations men have in Canada was their resemblance to sociability rather than intimate friendship. There is some evidence that working-class men prefer 'sociable leisure' that includes sociability rather than social integration (Perren et al. 2003: 79). These rural men fit into this category.

In addition, the men have internalized the western ethos of busyness. Keeping busy is a strategy that turns up in literature regarding aging transitions of all kinds, particularly retirement. It ties in with a belief in the benefits of activity to ward off decline or meaninglessness in old age that has been promoted since the Enlightenment. Activity theory has been at the centre of gerontological theorizing since the middle of the twentieth century, and a plethora of studies have concluded that being active in leisure or volunteer activities contributes to high morale among those who have undergone a major transition such as retirement or widowhood (Katz 2000).

It is not only professional gerontologists who believe in the importance of keeping busy, however. Widowers (and widows) frequently invoke the usefulness of keeping busy in order to overcome the challenges associated with both grieving and escaping from loneliness (Steeves & Kahn 2005). Rebecca M. Genoe (2004: 116) reports that her participants believed that:

'Keeping active was very important for their own well-being, and they also believed that other older men *should be encouraged* to keep their minds and bodies active' [emphasis added].

Similarly, Dorothy B. Crummy (2002: 60-61) notes that, for the widowers to whom she spoke, keeping busy was a way 'to avoid feelings of loneliness or self pity.' Consistent with the participants in this research, the men she interviewed 'credited keeping occupied with their ability to remain positive.' In fact, Robert Rubinstein (1986: 147) suggests that the keeping-busy philosophy is seen as 'a panacea for social and personal ills.' Rubinstein also notes that, 'activity can orient one outward' and, thereby, 'make a person's sense of aloneness and separateness disappear ... The implicit aloneness enshrined in 'living alone' is defended against' (217).

David Ekerdt (1986: 240, 243), in a seminal article, suggests that the 'busy ethic' has become, 'a logical part of people's attempt to manage a smooth transition from work to retirement.' Widowers use busyness to smooth their own transition, to get out of the house, and to escape from loneliness and melancholy. As well, in a society in which it is 'important to be busy,' staying busy is 'self-validating.'

Finally, the widowers embraced the independence and self-reliance that are part of masculinity. They argued that keeping busy is one's own responsibility. They emphasized their own agency in finding things to do and the importance of their activities' being spontaneous and premised on doing what they wanted to do when they wanted to do it.

This chapter has left out one major area of daily life, cooking and housework. I conceptualize these two chores as one area of activity for two reasons that are connected. First, cooking and house cleaning are the two tasks that are 'traditionally' the responsibility of wives, and second, the inability to carry out these feminine undertakings is one of the most common stereotypes about widowers. The next chapter addresses these two central components of widowers' everyday lives.

9 Cooking and Housework

When I tell people that I am doing a study about older men's experiences as widowers, they often comment that older men are not able to 'take care of themselves,' that is, cook, clean, and do laundry. These remarks reflect widely shared stereotypes about men's ability, or lack thereof, to survive on their own. This stereotype is not entirely fallacious. Lund, Caserta, and Diamond (1993: 246), for example, report that older men are 'deficient in a predictable set of skills, including cooking, shopping, and housecleaning.' Similarly, a study of household and marital roles (Keith 1994) found that majorities of older married men (those over 65) had never engaged in a variety of chores such as laundry and food preparation, while a significant minority had never cleaned, washed dishes, or gone shopping for household goods.

Many older widowers described traditionally feminine household tasks in ways that protected their sense of masculinity and emphasized that they were still 'real' men even though they had become competent at jobs traditionally thought of as women's work. Although most of the men had had at least some experience with cooking and/or housework as husbands, several brought up the stereotype of the man who 'does not even know how to boil water,' as a symbol of the widower who cannot take care of himself after his wife's death.

Cooking and housework came up in response to a variety of questions including the very broad first question that simply asked the participants to talk about their experience as widowers as well as to questions about what surprised them most and how they or their lives had changed. Some men did not bring up topics related to traditional 'women's work' until I did.

Older Widowers and Cooking

Alinde Moore and Dorothy Stratton (2002: 113), in their study of older widowers and resilience, note that cooking is 'a topic on which every man could comment.' The men I interviewed were equally likely to have something to say on the matter. Most knew how to cook at least a little. However, it is the way they talked about cooking in terms of their skill and attitudes towards it that shed light on its potential to undermine their sense of themselves as men at the same time that mastering cooking demonstrates a level of competence in an area that is not culturally defined as masculine.

The first indication that cooking was a skill men felt ambivalent about was when many, while admitting to knowing how to cook, felt the need to point out that their cooking was limited in some way. At the most basic level is the insistence that cooking is an issue of necessity rather than enjoyment. Al, for example, pointed out that eating is more about necessity than pleasure and likened his body to a machine:

I think your body is a machine that does need certain elements to feed it properly, just like an automobile does.

Herbert, in response to my asking if he did much cooking, said:

I cook for necessity ... Oh, I wouldn't starve, I'd cook.

Even though he makes it sound as if cooking is an unpleasant but necessary task, Herbert reported that he did cook 'biscuits and cakes.' Herbert had never tried baking bread, but he did have a bread machine:

I've never tried bread. I've got the instructions here. I've got a bread machine. *We had, my wife had it*, and I never used it. [emphasis added]

Note that Herbert changed the ownership of the bread maker from 'we' to 'my wife.' He was one of two men who emphasized the fact that this appliance was not theirs but their wives'. Chad explained that:

Well, I had a bread machine. *She* had one that she used to use, but I gave that to my daughter. [emphasis added]

Other widowers who knew how to cook for themselves clarified their skill by commenting that it was quite limited. They explained that they usually bought either canned or prepared food. Al, for example, characterized his cooking in the most minimal fashion:

> In emergencies, I even open a can of something for a meal.

A few men bought prepared foods or had them delivered. For example:

> I can't cook at all ... I eat well, I have Meals on Wheels[1]. . . And then I probably have soup. I can buy soup or cold meat or something ... or I go to M&M.[2] (Stephen)

> When I go for groceries, I buy a box of hamburgers already made up. (Herbert) [And have you learned to cook?] No. I buy finished meals ... I don't even want to learn how to cook ... all these pre-cooked meals are available. (Izzy)

Jacob explained that he cooked because he did not like eating in a restaurant by himself. However, as he went on to describe his cooking, it became clear that he also heated up food from cans:

> If I make soup, I make about six cans.

or uses prepared meals:

> I'm pretty fussy with my food. When I looked at food ... I found out the only place I can take food, down in B. [a nearby town]. I tried their prepared meals, but it wasn't that great.

Two men noted that even when they simply had to reheat food, they sometimes overcooked it to the point that it became inedible. For example:

> I can heat things up. Sometimes I overheat them, and they come out absolutely solid.

The men's insistence on their inability to learn how to cook food, or even to heat something from a can, is striking compared to the mastery with which they characterized most of their activities.

Several men who did know how to cook linked this traditionally feminine task with very masculine activities. Ralph, for example, talked about cooking during the war:

I do all my own cooking and everything, and I've had to for years. My mother, when I was a little boy, taught me how to cook and that came in handy ... Oh boy, I hated it with all my heart, but, boy even during the war when we were in certain situations ... even the commanding officer would come down and get a home-cooked meal. (Ralph)

Leroy learned how to cook because he was required not to marry during his first five years as a member of the Royal Canadian Mounted Police:

[Did you know how to cook before?] Oh yeah, a little bit. You know, I was a bachelor for five years before I got married ... when I joined the RCMP, you couldn't get married for five years ... I ate in restaurants ... but I did some cooking also, learned how to boil an egg and a few things.

Even though Leroy said he knew how to cook, he still minimized his skill by characterizing it as 'boiling eggs.' Stan likes to cook and points out that he learned to cook in the Navy while Patrick, a forester, learned to cook because:

I had to take care of myself when I was working because I was out in the woods camps and you just had to do your own cooking.

Marc was perhaps the most emphatic in associating his cooking with masculine activities. He explained that he really enjoys cooking, but he felt the need to complement his cooking ability with a list of his athletic activities:

Oh yeah, I enjoyed [cooking], enjoyed it really. And yet, despite the fact and I used to tell a lot of people, you know, I've played senior hockey, I've played senior basketball, I've played volley ball, I've played softball. Now, of course, I spent nine years coaching hockey at all the provincial levels. I coached baseball, you name it, and got involved with it and I'd say, 'hey, come on home; I'll cook you a steak.' So that to me was enjoyable; it still is enjoyable.

George remarked that he likes cooking, but followed up immediately by telling me that he is a bad housekeeper.[3]

Another strategy some men used was to describe their cooking as 'basic' or 'plain' in one way or another. Comments include:

My diet is really simple ... so I don't have to think about any elaborate cooking. (Winston)

So when I cook, it's nothing elaborate. Well, I grill some fish on the Foreman Grill or I'll put chicken breasts on the grill. Or I buy pork chops that they butterfly for me ... I put that on the grill. So, I mean, that's as far as I go. I don't make anything elaborate as far as meals go. It's very basic. (Ed)

There were several men who identified specific limitations. Matthew, for example, is a good cook, but he pointed out that he does not make pies or cakes. Angus suggested that, although he can cook, his cooking is very 'plain.' Nonetheless, his description of a holiday meal does not sound particularly simple or plain:

I mean I can cook a Christmas dinner. I mean I'm not into desserts or anything, but I can cook ... the vegetables and the creams ... cream sauces and all that sort of stuff, turkey with – I usually use oyster stuffing and make a nice dinner, you know. (Angus)

The widowers who knew how to cook indicated that they cook primarily 'masculine' things like turkeys, roasts, and meat and potatoes:

I make sure to cook a big dinner every night: meat and potatoes and all that stuff. Not so much pastries, not so much, but just meats and vegetables, this type of thing, the core of your meal. (Marc)

Almost no one admitted to making casseroles or desserts,[4] although a few men did have specialties that they prepared. Their specialties comprised seasonal food, and, therefore, did not encompass what one might consider the dishes of everyday cooking. For example, Stan made fruit cakes at Christmas time, and Ralph put up pickles every year. Several men talked about cooking on the Foreman Grill, which is not only promoted by a retired prize fighter but also replicates a barbeque, an appliance primarily used by men.

In contrast, there were a few men who affirmed that they were good cooks or liked cooking. For example, Grant described himself as the 'senior cook' in his marriage. Marcel, a European immigrant, had learned to cook in order to make the meals he remembered from his youth. Bernie, whose wife had been disabled, talked with pride about cooking for her. At the time of the interview, he had a girlfriend who:

keeps telling everybody what good cook I am. Actually, I'm not that great a cook, but there are certain dishes that, I'm great. I make a great stir fry. I love pasta and all variations of it. I love experimenting with sauces. I have a George Foreman Grill, and I love to make steaks ... I have no problem. I boil water, you know ... I enjoy watching the cooking channel ...

Bernie's friend was disabled and had trouble swallowing. He took great pride in making 'all kinds of soft dishes ... for her.' Thus, 'agency speech' (Kirsi et al. 2000: 161) accompanied the self-deprecating language. In addition, because Bernie had a girlfriend, he may have felt less pressure to minimize his competence in the area of cooking.[5] Bernie summed up his comments by pointing out that he knew how to boil water, a task that was obviously well below his skill level. Even he felt the need to counterbalance his bragging about his ability to cook with a minimizing statement, 'I boil water.' Not knowing how to boil water is symbolic of the inability of men to take care of themselves.

Bernie and Grant were not the only widowers who talked about cooking with a sense of competence and pride. Marc, in addition to embedding his remarks about his ability to cook in a list of his sporting activities, jokingly challenged me to a 'cook-off' bringing a component of competition into his description while a few compared their ability to cook with men who could not cook:[6]

You know, a friend of ours ... he didn't do any of that. And his wife died three or four years ago. Well, he had a hard time because he never got himself a meal. (Bob)

Nobody tells widowers how to get along, how to cook for one. Most of these men I talk to have no idea how to cook. I said, 'My God, there's nothing to it.' (Matthew)

Angus explained that a lot of widowers rush to remarry because:

They can't boil water or think they can't, and they own a house and, my goodness.

Ed, who had been in business with his wife and said they shared the housework, saw competence in the areas of cooking and housework as elements of self-sufficiency and identified it as 'one of the most important things other people should know about widowhood' (interview question):

> To make sure you're self-sufficient ... not to feel lost ... We shared those
> things all our life. So there's nothing new to me, but there's some men
> who've never done that.

Jacob summed up learning to cook bluntly, saying, 'I just learned.'

One widower's comments about cooking stand out, and it is noteworthy that, not only was he younger than the other widowers (in his
late 40s when his wife died), but he also had children still living at
home at that time. Leonard gave a moving account of his teenaged
daughter watching cooking shows on television to take up some of the
roles of a 'mother' to the family. Leonard had had a 'pretty traditional
relationship' with his wife, but he joined his daughter and has since
learned to enjoy cooking. Cooking for Leonard was also a way of recreating the home his family lost through the death of his wife:

> And I found a book that my wife had started ...[with] all the recipes that she
> made that everybody liked. So that was such a gift ... And I started baking
> the same muffins and all the smells came back into the house ... and that
> was really good because it kind of put the smells back into the house and
> the warmth back into the house ... So I think that opened up cooking for me
> that wouldn't have any other way, I think. And I really enjoyed it.

Recall that Leonard had described his sense of unease in his house after
his wife died. Bringing back the smells of her cooking into the house
made it once more livable for Leonard and his children.

The widowers' discussion of cooking brings together observations
that other writers have made. Notable is the embedding of talk about
cooking into a masculine context. First is the conceptualizing of one's
body as a machine. Moss and colleagues (2007), in their article about
frail men's perspectives on food, also noted that some of the men
they talked to equated their bodies to a machine and food as fuel for
their machine. Toni Calasanti (2004: 308) has suggested that this approach to one's body is 'a way to affirm manhood to athletes and
nonathletes alike.'

Similarly, several of the men who knew how to cook looked to manly
social contexts in order to explain why they knew about cooking. They
invoked sports, the military, and serving in the Royal Canadian
Mounted Police in order to justify their proficiency at this most feminine task. Moore and Stratton (2002) also noted that the widowers they

interviewed raised similar issues as well as having learned how to cook as a child which the men in this study also mentioned.

Ribeiro, Paúl, and Nogueira (2007), in a study of Portugese men who were caring for their wives, observe that their participants 'conveniently' included references to 'previous life experiences' that embody masculinity in their description of caring tasks. We can see in the wording used by some of the widowers that they, similarly, slip in references to sports or the military in an almost by-the-way fashion.

The participants' comments about other types of housework are more straightforward. There are two themes that emerge: (1) buying the housework and (2) having a lower standard of cleanliness than their wives. Kate Davidson commented that the British men she interviewed also said that they did not keep up their houses to the standards of their wives and saw housework as something that 'had to be done' (1999: 120).

Cleaning and Laundry

As mentioned above, there were several men who avoided the need to cook by buying prepared meals or subscribing to Meals on Wheels. Buying housekeeping was another strategy the men used. Tim, in addition to subscribing to Meals on Wheels, for example, used 'home care' that included housekeeping and cooking:

> I get home care; the girls come in two hours a day ... five days a week, and do my housework for me. And if I've got any cooking, they'll do that.

Leroy remarked:

> I have a housekeeper that comes in about every second week, and she swabs the floor out and vacuums and changes my bed, and *I don't know what she does*. Dusts and does fooling around, you know. She stays about two, two and a half hours ... and cleans me all up and washes the windows, or *whatever she wants to do*. [emphasis added]

Leroy simply relies on his housekeeper to maintain standards of cleanliness around the house. He does not even pretend to know what needs to be done and adopts the language of sailors – for example, 'swabs the floor,' in the description of what the housekeeper does. This housekeeper started working for Leroy and his wife while his wife was ill. After she died:

She just carried right on.

Stephen, who is 91 years old, depended on his daughter to arrange both Meals on Wheels and housekeeping for him:

I have a very nice woman who comes in two days a week. In the morning, two or three hours, two mornings a week. She's extremely good. She keeps the place in good condition, cleaning and that sort of thing. And she's a person that I can talk to.

Stephen depends on the home-care worker not only to carry out the feminine tasks of housework, but also to conform to the wifely role of being a listening ear for him.

Hiring a housekeeper in Florida is quite common and often unrelated to physical ability or marital status. Al used to hire a housekeeper, but:

I used to have people come in and do the housework. But things started disappearing.[7] So I stopped it. Now I do my own work. It's not too good, but I do a little here and there, and I get by. I don't think the house is dirty. It may be a little messy, but it's not dirty. I do one room at a time – do the dusting and vacuuming and whatnot.

Al's description of his housekeeping skills is characteristic of the way many widowers talk about doing their own housework. They do the work, but they insist that they have a fairly low standard of cleanliness (Moore and Stratton 2002; Davidson 1999).

George and Samuel provided the most extreme descriptions of poor housekeeping. George, in our phone conversation while making the interview appointment, was adamant that we not meet in his home because it was too messy. He described such a degree of disarray that it sounded like an obstacle course. Samuel associated his lack of housekeeping or caring about it with the early days of widowhood when everything in his life seemed meaningless:

The days seemed to be meaningless. I just seemed to be passing the time ... I wasn't making progress in cleaning the house because I never bothered cleaning the house ... I eat simply and I never had any trouble cooking. Uh, I was very neglectful about the house ... If someone would come to visit me, I would clean it up as best I can. But I wouldn't do as good a job as a cleaning lady would ... I really didn't, didn't care at all about what the house looked like. It was really a mess ... Of course, I'm generalizing, but one of the things about men is that they're not as fussy about the house as women.

Samuel, who spent most of his energy trying to find a girlfriend during his early days of widowhood, has since married. He remarked that because he had found a girlfriend:

I have a cleaning lady coming here now ... Things are different now.

Even several men who did claim some ability to keep their houses clean still pointed out that their standard was lower than their wives'. Chad, for example, did all his own housework and 'helped' his wife when she was alive. His comments communicated the superficiality of his knowledge about house cleaning, the everyday nature of the work as onerous, and the lack of satisfaction he got from doing it:

I do housework stuff. I do all my own vacuuming. I've got a big central vacuuming system in there, and all that stuff. I've done all that stuff before and laundry stuff. There are some things that I got: two shelves full of chemicals in there. *I don't know what the hell she used that for,* but I'm going to throw them out one of these days ... My clothes are probably not as clean as they should be, but I wash them ... I have a shirt hanging on the doorknob that's been there for two weeks now waiting. Now I've got to sew buttons on it, but I keep putting it off ... I'm starting to get a little bit tired of housework and all that stuff ... You know, I don't always do a good job of it. Sometimes I just give it a lick and a promise every couple of weeks. [emphasis added]

A few participants saw housework as part of the discipline of getting on with life, developing a routine, and keeping busy. Two men conceptually linked housework with work around their property, another way of minimizing the feminine nature of what they were doing.

Several men commented that they had had no idea about how much work went into keeping up the house, whether in terms of having to plan what to eat for supper every night or just in terms of the amount of work involved. Keith's remarks are particularly poignant:

> I guess I was spoiled ... I used to help her out once in a while ... but the one thing I really regret is that I didn't help her out enough around the house because I never realized the amount of work to keep a house going until afterwards ... It's amazing, just the towels. Surprising, the lint off the towels ... You clean the bathroom one day and have a shower the next. And the lint off the towels, you have to dust again, you know ... Or just a little lunch, you know. There's a mess. You've got to wash the dishes and stuff like that. It's the planning that always gets me...[Is there anything that particularly surprised you about being a widower?] No, it's just that I never realized that there was so much work to keeping a house going, you know. Just to keep it clean, half decent... that's what I regret most. I never helped her enough, you know. Around the house anyway.

Keith is referring to what Mason calls 'sentient care,' activities wives perform that are so taken for granted by their husbands that they are virtually invisible. Only after the women are no longer around to perform these activities do widowers recognize the extent of this work (Mason 1996 cited in Davidson et al. 2000: 543).

A possible preview of the future is the reaction of the men who talked about sharing housework because both they and their wives were in the work place. The most striking comments came from Ed, who had been in business with his wife. He and his wife seem to have truly shared responsibility for cooking and housework. Nonetheless, Ed's wife was still the expert. Ed said that when he and his wife were both working:

> Whoever got home first would start supper. [My wife] taught me very well. She taught me to be self-sufficient in the house ... Taught me how to clean the house, to make the beds, do the wash. But, like I said, we were in business so we shared everything ... It wasn't, well, you know, 'I'm the man of the house. You've got to do everything else.' No, we shared all the chores ... it was an equal partnership.

Even though Ed talked about housework and cooking as if the situation had been truly equal, he noted that, after his wife's death, he had to learn to do food shopping. Ed hated this task and had left it to his wife. In addition to doing 'basic' cooking, Ed explained that:

> Once in while, I get ambitious. I clean; I do housework.

Although a couple of the men did fit into the stereotype of the old man who is incapable of taking care of himself, most had known at least a little about these tasks before their wives' deaths. They may have found satisfaction by favourably comparing themselves to other men who did not know how to clean, cook, or even 'boil water.'

Even more striking than the diversity of these older widowers' comments about the level of their skill in cooking and cleaning is the ambivalence with which they discussed these topics and their efforts to intersperse evidence of their masculinity as part of their observations. They ensured that any listener would understand that they cooked plain, masculine food rather than casseroles or desserts; that they knew how to clean, but not too well.

One cannot help but interpret the men's discussion of household tasks as an example of impression management (Goffman 1959). They worked very hard to demonstrate that cooking and cleaning were difficult, if not impossible, for them to master. In almost every other area of life that they described, the men made efforts to appear confident and in control. Only feminine tasks were beyond their capacity to master.

In addition, several of the men indicated that the major problem of housework for them was its everyday nature. Day in, day out, the towels dropped lint all over the bathroom, and someone, now they, had to decide what to make for supper. In the past, even if the men had helped their wives, their participation had been secondary (Gerson and Peiss 1985), and they had depended on their wives' expertise. Once they became widowers, the men had to take over the women's work that their wives had always done, and there is evidence that men who are widowed do spend considerably more time on 'female-typed tasks' than married men (South and Spitze 1994: 343). In fact, Sanjiv Gupta (1999) has found that men's housework time increases by 61 per cent when they leave co-habitation or marriage, particularly time spent doing female-typed chores. Because such work is so heavily gendered, the men made obvious efforts to show that cooking and cleaning are not a part of their essential nature as men.

There is some indication that men are slowly beginning to view feminine household chores as less challenging to their sense of themselves as men. We have seen, in this chapter, one man who had worked as business partner with his wife take some pride in knowing how to cook and clean, albeit with his wife as the expert who took over the food shopping because he did not want to do it. As well, the youngest widower in the group had found real satisfaction in learning how to cook his wife's specialties and in recreating a 'home' for himself and his children. Only time will tell to what extent men will cease to see cleaning and cooking as women's work and, therefore not to be mastered.[8]

10 Conclusion

What is the foreign country like, into which men are thrust when their wives die? How do widowers manage to navigate when they arrive there? As we have seen, most of these men were totally unprepared for their lives as widowers. They had expected to die before their wives and had few role models. Even when they knew that their wives were dying, there was no reference group with which they could begin to identify as their initiation as widowers approached. When their wives died, they were thrust into the land of singlehood.

A few men referred to themselves as bachelors or saw themselves simply as single. They talked about being 'free' in ways that we might envision a young bachelor to be unencumbered and attempted to build a new life on a foundation of busyness and low levels of commitment. In some ways, the widowers tried to go back to the place they remembered from their pre-marriage days as young men. Unfortunately, neither they nor the social landscape was the same as it had been.

The men did not talk about the past a great deal except for discussions about their work lives. Nonetheless, one gets the feeling from their stories that they were nostalgic for a past as single men that may never have existed. These older widowers fell back into familiar masculine habits and conjured up images of youth when rebuilding their lives. They also used masculine images when they talked about their experiences. As Gabriela Spector-Mercel (2006) has pointed out, there are no social scripts available for older men to use. Hence, the masculine images the widowers relied on were borrowed from those of their youth. They used these images to provide fragments of masculinity which would allow them to develop a mosaic that they could achieve.

How does this situation affect the way the men talked about different aspects of their experiences associated with widowhood?

A major theme that runs through this book is the participants' reluctance to elaborate on areas of their lives that had a considerable emotional component. This reluctance meant that although they were more than willing to talk at length about their previous occupations or their participation in sports, they tended to skate over discussions of what it was like when their wives were dying or how a romantic relationship with a new woman developed once they had started seeing one another.

Although the men undoubtedly gave personal care to their wives and experienced strong emotions associated with grieving, many, particularly the Canadian widowers, were unable or unwilling to emphasize these aspects of their experience. Differences between the more reserved Atlantic Canadian, rural or semi-rural culture and the more direct, demonstrative Jewish, urban culture were obvious in the men's ways of talking about this period of their lives. The Canadian widowers exhibited a stoic approach, while the American, Jewish group used a rich vocabulary of emotions when they described how they felt around the time of their wives' deaths.

Both groups communicated their love for their wives by describing their competence as husbands. They concentrated on things like renovating their houses in a way that would please their wives. Similarly, their approaches to arranging a funeral and completing paperwork reflected their capacity to organize and plan.

In terms of the funeral, most striking were the decisions by several men not to follow their wives' wishes. As well, they (similar to widows) for the most part found the size of the turnout at the funeral to be as or more important than the content of the funeral itself. Particularly meaningful were crowds that were larger than expected. The presence of so many friends and colleagues communicated respect and affection for their wives that was very gratifying for the husbands.

When the widowers began talking about their relationships, it became clear that their wives had been intermediaries on whom they depended for maintaining and setting the tone with their children and with friends. Their children had confided in their mothers, who often had had the responsibility for keeping in touch. The men and children had known how to interact when there was a mother around. Whether the relationship had been good or bad, it was the mother who had set its tone.

Once the mothers of these children had died, things became more complicated. The nature of the interactions and feelings between the widowers and their children no longer conformed to what we usually see in relationships between older fathers and their adult children. Daughters who were expected to be uncritical sometimes stepped into the shoes of the adult woman in the family, whose job it is to monitor and control the behaviour of the men. When this happened, the widowers reacted quite strongly. Often, the bone of contention was a widower is beginning to move towards developing a couple relationship with a new woman.

Dealings with women were fraught with difficulty and uncertainty. In general, the men saw finding 'someone' as only natural even when they, themselves, were not interested. For the most part, they did not consider friendships with women viable and interpreted any approach by a woman as an attempt to develop a couple relationship. Particularly for the Atlantic-Canadian widowers, the desire to be in control led to their rejection of both matchmaking and women who appeared to be actively trying to attract their attention.

Although the men expressly stated that they wanted to be in control of initiating a couple relationship, their description of how the original attraction evolved into a more serious relationship reflected a singular lack of agency. While the Florida widowers recounted forward behaviour on the part of their 'friends,' the Canadian widowers used phrases like, 'one thing led to another' to describe the development of these connections.

Often the men did not seem to play an active role in the continuation or lack thereof of their friendships with couples or with other men. Here again, it was their wives who had been primarily responsible for maintaining friendship bonds. Some men explained that their friendships had faded away in a fashion that they saw as natural. Being the 'fifth wheel' in a couples' world was not comfortable, and both the widowers and the members of the other couples let their friendships evaporate without much thought. In these cases, the men did not seem to have a strong reaction to the loss. They saw it as an inevitable part of the transition to widowhood.

Other men had stronger feelings. They felt let down by the failure of their friends to keep up with them. Some reacted by deciding that the friends had really been their wives' friends. It is impossible to know if they were correct in this interpretation. Interestingly, women, when deserted by friends as a result of becoming widowed, similarly believe that the friends' attachment had been primarily to the other spouse (van den Hoonaard 2001). It may be that the discomfort that friends feel when interacting with the half of a couple who is left is similar whether the person who died is a man or a woman. They cannot recreate the pattern of interaction or are too uncomfortable with a grieving spouse and would cease being friends regardless of which spouse died (Lopata 1996: 160).

Most of the widowers either would not or could not participate in friendship in ways that would encourage the maintenance of close connections. Most neither invited people to their homes nor confided in their friends. As well, they tended to avoid ongoing commitments with friends and/or acquaintances. Some became very proficient at running into neighbours or acquaintances at coffee shops, snowmobile runs, or at the pool in a retirement community. The ad hoc nature of their relationships contributed to a sense of independence and freedom that the widowers cherished at the same time that it discouraged ongoing, intimate relationships.

The men not only had to learn to relate to people in their social world in new ways; they also felt different in their own houses. Unlike many women who learn to enjoy living alone, the widowers found the solitude of being home alone almost intolerable. 'Getting out' became an essential component of their lives. It represented the ability to continue with one's life and to succeed at being a busy person. Comments that suggested that remaining at home symbolized giving up and dwelling on one's unfortunate situation appeared throughout the interviews.

The home-based activities that we associate with women's work, cooking and cleaning, remained unnatural activities for the widowers. They felt the need to underline the strangeness of these activities and their lack of ability or interest to develop a competence that was adequate or more than adequate. Harvey C. Mansfield, in *Manliness*, has commented that: '[Men do not] look down on [women's work] because they think it is dirty or boring or insignificant, which is often true of men's work; they look down on it because it is women's' (2006: 8).

Research on fathering echoes the desire for men to distance themselves from work that we identify as women's work. Annette Lareau (2000: 428) for example, found that, when she interviewed fathers, they did not seem to know very much about the day-to-day details of their children's lives but 'excelled' at talking about 'their own work experiences, their leisure activities, and masculinity.'

These observations of widowers are contemporary and, therefore contradict the reaction I often hear that times have changed. People comment that the men whose stories appear in this book are 'old.' Surely, things have changed, and future generations of widowers will not have the same gender-based challenges to face. Surely, future widowers will already know how to cook and clean and will be less attached to traditional masculinity. What does the future hold for older men's experiences and their ways of talking about them?

Although changes in the way men and women relate and in the shape of marriage (and other forms of 'partnering') have altered in profound ways over the last forty years, I would suggest that things have not changed as much as we think or might like. Young men's lives are very different, however, from those of their fathers and grandfathers.

Where Do We Go from Here?

Most people with whom I have spoken about this book suggested that men in the future will not manifest masculinity to the same extent as the widowers whom I interviewed, that the gender issues will have diminished or disappeared. After all, today's men spend more time taking care of their children and taking care of their homes. The gender issues will simply not be as prominent as they have been for the men who are old today. I would argue, however, that although things have changed, we overestimate the impact of those changes.

As Arlie Hochschild found in the late 1980s in *The Second Shift* (1989), women still shouldered the responsibility for childcare and housework. When men appear to share these tasks, they are often simply continuing to do the masculine work, cutting the lawn, for instance, or taking their children to the zoo. Anthony McMahon (1999) argues that men continue to do less housework and refrain from taking domestic responsibility because it is in their interest not to. He suggests that the 'rhetoric of optimistic gradualism' is simply one more way that men avoid leaving masculinity behind. There may be truth to this suggestion. Recently, Andrea Doucet in *Do Men Mother?* (2007) has noted that even when married fathers are the primary caregivers of their children, housework often remains a very sensitive issue.

Still, much has changed. Both men and women are leaving their parents' homes before marriage. Living alone has become much more common for adults of all ages. Statistics Canada (2003: 2) has noted that, 'By 2001, 13% of the population aged 15 and older lived alone compared with 9% in 1981.' These numbers reflect both the phenomenon of older persons', especially older women's, living alone as well as the return of some adult children, often referred to as 'boomerang children' (Connidis 2001: 156). It also includes men who live alone after marriage breakdown. These phenomena represent a lack of stability within the economy and within families.

The statistics tell us that when older men of the future become widowers, they will likely have lived alone for at least part of their adult lives. We might assume that this means that they will be more comfortable with cooking and housework. However, as we see in media reports, more and more adults, women and men, are relying on prepared food rather than learning how to cook themselves. Housework continues to be defined as women's work – men continue to bolster their sense of masculinity by minimizing their competence in these areas.

While some men have become more involved in childcare and perhaps closer to their children, there has also been a trend towards unstable relationships with the increase in the prevalence of divorce and couples deciding not to marry at all. Does this mean that many men will have even more distant relationships with their children than today's older widowers whose wives mediated their relationships?

When we look at changes in gender norms, it appears that we are much more comfortable with women adopting so-called masculine ways of being than we are with men becoming more like women. Women have entered the labour force in huge numbers, but men have opted to be stay-at-home fathers only in small numbers. Girls may play boys' sports, but we do not see boys being encouraged to play with dolls and kitchen sets.

As I write this conclusion, the Canadian Broadcasting Corporation (CBC) is airing a 'reality' show, *The Week the Women Went*, on television. The show, which takes place in a small town in Alberta, rests on the following premise: '*The Week the Women Went* finds out what happens when the women of a town are whisked off for a week-long vacation with little to no contact with their families. The men are left to their own devices, juggling school lunches, homework and housework, in addition to jobs, businesses, and running the town' (Canadian Broadcasting Corporation: 2008).

The question of whether or not men can take care of themselves arises frequently throughout the episodes. The show portrays many of the men as incompetent at taking care of their children and seeming not to know how to run their households. The women, who are supposedly on vacation at a posh resort, remain unconvinced and anxious about leaving their children and homes solely in the hands of their husbands, ex-husbands, and boyfriends.[1]

The mystique of being single and free when there are no women to constrain their activities (which the widowers invoked) is one of the first themes of this show. When their wives depart for the week, the men immediately leave for the golf course and arrange barbecues. We see them lounging around, sipping beer, and laughing boisterously. The show provides an eerie resemblance to the stereotypes mentioned in this book and to the ways some men described themselves and their lives as widowers.

Final Thoughts

When I first started working on this book, I chose a tentative title, *By Himself*, which I expected would change as I collected data and analysed them. The title turned out to fit very well because the widowers whose stories I collected did, indeed, focus on their competence as independent actors in most areas of their lives. They went to great lengths to explain their self-reliance in rebuilding lives that may have been very lonely but also reflected a desire for minimal commitments. The men wanted to call the shots regarding what they did and with whom they did it. In some ways, the widowers were living in a new country in the manner of ex-patriates. They had learned how to navigate an unfamiliar social context while refraining from changing either their sense of self or approach to everyday life. To maintain their self-concept as real men, the widowers refrained from colonizing the new land and, like expatriates, were attempting to return to a life that may or may not have ever existed.

Appendix: Interview Guide

- Where and when were you born? How long were you married? Occupation?
- What's it like being a widower?
- How did your wife die?
- Would you tell me something about the funeral? Your most vivid memories of the early days?
- How would you say your life has changed since your wife died?
- What has been the most difficult aspect of your life since her death?
- Anything that particularly surprised you?
- Have you ever lived alone before?
- What have you done with your wife's things?
- How has your relationship between you and your children changed since your wife died?
- Has your relationship between you and your friends changed? How?
- What are the most important things that other people should know about the experience of being a widower?
- Do you remember the first time somebody referred to you or you thought of yourself as a widower? Does the word widower conjure up an image for you?
- How would you say you have changed since your wife died?
- Do you think you might consider remarrying?
- (If widower is in a couple relationship) How do your children feel about this relationship?
- Is there any time that is particularly challenging for you?
- Do you go to church very often? Has your faith made a difference?
- Have you gone for any kind of counselling?
- Anything that I should have asked you that I didn't?

Notes

1 Introduction

1 Given the rather small population in each of the Atlantic Provinces, it is necessary not to identify the specific province in order to protect the confidentiality of the men I interviewed.

2 Although Berardo's article (1970) is over thirty years old, it continues to be cited regularly because there is so little else to refer to. When I met Felix Berardo in 2002, he commented that he was very surprised that the article continues to appear so frequently in literature reviews.

3 See the Appendix for a version of the interview guide.

4 Acadians make up the French-speaking population in the Atlantic Provinces.

5 This categorization of people is so pervasive that T.K. Pratt (1982) reported that on his second day living on Prince Edward Island, 'I met a small girl with a black dog. "That's a nice dog," I said. "You from away?" she replied instantly.' It also underlines the deep awareness of the importance of being either an Islander or from away. Even the youngest locals have internalized this distinction.

6 Tim Horton's is a coffee shop named after a Canadian hockey player. Tim's is pervasive and sees itself, and is seen, as an integral part of Canadian culture. In the small city of 50,000 in which I live, there are no fewer than ten Tim Horton's, all of which are always busy.

7 The material in the next few paragraphs is adapted from van den Hoonaard (1992), *The Aging of a Florida Retirement Community*.

8 In fact, in reading a student's dissertation about academic writing, I was able to identify someone even though the student had changed the gender,

the province and the academic discipline. Maintaining confidentiality in this social context is a real challenge.

9 See van den Hoonaard (2009b) for a discussion of the challenges of masculinity for old men.

10 Unless otherwise noted, 'widowers' refers to the men I studied for this book. Their experiences and perceptions do not necessarily reflect those of all widowers.

2 Masculinity and Older Widowers

1 'Do you remember the first time that somebody called you a widower or you thought of yourself as a widower?'

2 Unless otherwise stated, all quotations in this book are taken verbatim from the interviews. All the widowers' names are pseudonyms, and I have changed minor details about their lives when necessary to maintain the confidentiality of the participants.

3 See van den Hoonaard (1997) for a discussion of the 'identity foreclosure' that women often experience.

4 'Do you remember the first time that somebody called you a widower or you thought of yourself as a widower?'

5 See Chapter Five for a discussion of men's noticing that women seem to treat them differently and make a fuss over them. This leads some men to believe that they are being pursued aggressively by women who are looking for a romantic involvement.

3 Becoming a Widower

1 It is noteworthy that the participants did not refer to themselves as caregivers. Others have also found (e.g., Davidson 1999) that both husbands and wives do not think of the caring they do for sick spouses as caregiving or themselves as caregivers. Rather, they see these activities as simply part of their roles as spouses.

2 Crummy (2002: 59) identifies 'doing what you have to do' as one of the major themes in her study of widowers and resilience. She commented that, 'Such an attitude seemed to stem from [the participants'] very being, and was an expectation that they had for themselves.'

3 Davidson et al. (2000: 545) report that the widowers in their study also said that their wives never or hardly complained.

4 The phrase, 'heroic measures,' was used only by the Florida widowers.

4 Early Days of Widowhood

1 *Shiva* is the seven days of mourning following a death in the Jewish tradition. It can include sitting on low stools and tearing one's clothes. For the less observant, it may simply entail the family's being together in one place where friends can visit and express their condolences.

2 Stephen was also the oldest widower in the study (91 at the time of our interview). His age may also have had a role in his desire to rely on his children for arranging their mother's funeral as well as other aspects of his life, for example, housekeeping.

3 Widows also place great importance on how many people attended their husband's funeral (van den Hoonaard 2001).

5 Widowers' Relationships with Their Children

1 Children in this case refers to the adult children of the widowers.

2 It was clear from the context that Ralph is talking about extramarital affairs here.

6 Women in the Lives of Widowers

1 Although the term 'repartnering' is used throughout the literature on developing a couple relationship after becoming widowed, the participants never used this term themselves. This may reflect a cohort effect – the practice of calling one's spouse, live-in, or steady person a 'partner' is fairly recent.

2 George had lived alone for the last four years of his marriage. His wife, who had Alzheimer's Disease, resided in a nursing home for that period.

3 His second wife died about three years before our interview.

4 See van den Hoonaard (2001) for a discussion of women's staying single as a way of remaining loyal to their husbands.

5 See Chapter Six for a discussion of widowers' relationships with friends. These relationships tend to be activity based, require little commitment, and entail little, if any, confiding.

6 This fear is not unfounded. When I interviewed women about widowhood, several talked about the challenge of interpreting men's intentions (see van den Hoonaard 2001).

7 Herbert is speaking here of a specific approach rather than to Christianity broadly. He commented that it is possible to be both a Catholic and a 'Christian.'

8 In fact, playwright Robert John Ford (2006) has written a play called 'The Casserole Brigade,' about a group of widows who make casseroles in order to attract eligible widowers.

9 The legend of lonely, aggressive widows is widespread. When people hear about my research, they regularly tell me stories of men who were chased by women. One of my favourites includes a widower who found a woman in his bed!

10 It is important to recognize that most people who live in this retirement community live far from their children. Thus, members of the community often depend on one another for help, like driving each other to the doctor or airport, that widowers in Atlantic Canada might depend on their children to provide. Residents of this community characterize this situation that contributes to a value of mutual helpfulness as 'all being in the same boat' (van den Hoonaard 1992).

11 Karlsson and Borell (2004: 3) note that the term LAT is primarily a European one. In North America, this type of relationship has not been named, and interview participants use terms borrowed from youth culture, e.g., 'going steady,' to describe their intimate connections. As seen in Chapter One, widowers adopt the youth-culture term 'bachelor' to refer to themselves.

12 In contrast, European authors who write about LAT relationships, comment that it is usually the women who do not want to live in the same household with men (Karlsson and Borell 2004; Stevens 2004).

7 Relationships with Friends

1 In my studies of women's experiences of widowhood (van den Hoonaard 1997, 2001), I found that several authors suggested that lost friends had really been their husbands,' rather than their, friends.

2 Ed is correct in his assumption that his experience is unusual (van den Hoonaard 1994). His friendships do fit the pattern of the single person's accompanying couple friends rather than initiating outings.

8 Everyday Life in and out of the House

1 See Chapter Five for an explanation of the men's propensity to have a 'current woman' (Moore and Stratton 2002) who would accompany them to social events.

2 In fact, Charles's impression is not entirely borne out in research. See van den Hoonaard (1994) for a discussion of widows' social lives in retirement communities.

3 In Atlantic Canada, as in many rural and semi-rural social contexts, people who were not born there are considered to have 'come from away' even if they moved to the area as children and have lived there for their entire lives. Those who arrive as adults are always outsiders to some extent.

4 The other categories include: media consumers, culture enthusiasts, and sophisticated choosers.

5 See Chapter Five for a discussion of the widowers' concerns about being sought by women whom they perceived to want a committed relationship.

6 'We-Care' is a volunteer driving service that is organized in one of the larger retirement communities that is nearby.

7 In the Florida retirement communities where these men lived, helping out one's neighbours is a strong norm (see van den Hoonaard 1992).

8 The Seder is the ritual meal that takes place at the beginning of Passover.

9 The first place is home, and the second place is work. (Oldenburg 1989: 16)

9 Cooking and Housework

1 One other man also subscribed to 'Meals on Wheels' because as a diabetic he needs to be very careful with his diet. This service delivers meals once a day at noon. Some people buy two meals in order to cover their supper or save some of the midday meal to eat later on.

2 M&M is a store that sells prepared meals that one can simply warm up.

3 George was the only man I did not interview in his home. He claimed that his house was so messy that I might hurt myself if I tried to navigate through the rooms.

4 As an interesting aside, single women who some widowers perceive to be chasing them are often characterized by the men as arriving on the doorstop bearing casseroles. For example, John Bayley (2001: 3) opens his memoire of his life as a widower this way: 'Now eat it while it's nice and hot,' ordered Margot, putting a large lump of casserole on my plate.

5 My thanks to Ms Marianne Skarborn of Fredericton, New Brunswick, who brought this to my attention.

6 These descriptions of men who have no idea how to cook are reminiscent of the way widows who participated in an earlier study (see van den Hoonaard 2001) talked about women who 'didn't even know how to write a cheque.'

7 In Florida retirement communities, many people hire immigrants from Haiti or Cuba and do not share a language with them. The social distance is thus immense, and the terminology I have heard people use in the pool area to refer to their housekeepers provides a clue that these two groups

have an 'us-and-them' relationship that might contribute to distrust and exploitation between them.

8   Some have observed that today's young people, both men and women, are not learning how to cook as a result of the combination of the demise of the family meal and the widespread use of convenience food.

10 Conclusion

1   My own daughter, who is the mother of two small children, has expressed surprise at how many of her female friends are afraid to leave their young children with their husbands for fear that they would not be able to care for the children competently.

References

Adams, R.G. (1994). Older Men's Friendship Patterns. In E.H. Thompson (Ed.), *Older Men's Lives*, 159–77. Thousand Oaks: Sage.

Adams, R.G. (1985). People Would Talk: Normative Barriers to Cross-Sex Friendship for Elderly Women. *Gerontologist* 25(6): 605–11.

Adams, R.G., Blieszner, R., and de Vries, B. (2000). Definitions of Friendship in the Third Age: Age, Gender, and Study Location Effects. *Journal of Aging Studies* 14(1): 117–33.

Aléx, L., Hammarström, A., Norberg, A., and Lundman, B. (2008). Construction of Masculinities among Men Aged 85 and Older in the North of Sweden. *Journal of Clinical Nursing* 17: 451–59.

Allan, G.A. (1979). *A Sociology of Friendship and Kinship*. London: George Allen and Unwin.

Arber, S., Price, D., Davidson, K., and Perren, K. (2003). Re-examining Gender and Marital Status: Material Well-Being and Social Involvement. In S. Arber, K. Davidson, and J. Ginn (Eds.), *Gender and Ageing: Changing Roles and Relationships*, 148–67. Philadelphia: Maidenhead Press.

Auger, J.A. (2000). *Social Perspectives on Death and Dying*. Halifax: Fernwood.

Bayley, J. (2001). *Widower's House: A Study in Bereavement or How Margot and Mella Forced Me to Flee My Home*. New York: Norton.

Becker, H.S. (1998). *Tricks of the Trade: How to Think about Your Research While You're Doing It*. Chicago: University of Chicago Press.

Becker, H.S. (1996). The Epistemology of Qualitative Research. In R. Jessor, A. Colby, and R. Schweder (Eds.), *Essays on Ethnography and Human Development*, 53–71. Chicago: University of Chicago Press.

Bennett, K.M. (2007). 'No Sissy Stuff': Towards a Theory of Masculinity and Emotional Expression in Older Widowed Men. *Journal of Aging Studies* 21(4): 347–56.

Bennett, K.M. (2005). 'Was Life Worth Living?' Older Widowers and Their Explicit Discourses of the Decision to Live. *Mortality* 10(2): 144–54.

Bernard, J. (1995) [1981]. The Good-Provider Role: Its Rise and Fall. In M.S. Kimmel and M.A. Messner (Eds.), *Men's Lives.* 3rd ed., 149–63. Boston: Allyn and Bacon.

Bernard, J. (1973). *The Future of Marriage.* New York: Bantam.

Berardo, F.M. (1970) Survivorship and Social Isolation: The Case of the Aged Widower. *Family Coordinator* 19: 11–15.

Binstock, R.H. (1985). The Oldest Old: A Fresh Perspective or Compassionate Ageism Revisited? *Milbank Memorial Fund Quarterly / Health and Society* 63(2): 420–51.

Bird, S.R. (1996). Welcome to the Men's Club: Homosociality and the Maintenance of Hegemonic Masculinity. *Gender and Society* 10(2): 120–32.

Blau, Z.S. (1961). Structural Constraints on Friendships in Old Age. *American Sociological Review* 26: 429–39.

Bleiszner, R.G., and de Vries, B. (2000). Definitions of Friendship in the Third Age: Gender Location Effects. *Journal of Aging Studies* 14(1): 117–33.

Bottoms, D. (1996). The Widower (Poem). *Poetry* 168(5): 270.

Brandth, B., and Haugen, M.S. (2005). Doing Rural Masculinity– From Logging to Outfield Tourism. *Journal of Gender Studies* 14(1): 13–22.

Brannon, R. (1976). The Male Sex Role: And What It's Done for Us Lately. In R. Brannon and D. Davids (Eds.), *The Forty-Nine Percent Majority,* 1–40. Reading: Addison-Wesley.

Calasanti, T. (2004). Feminist Gerontology and Old Men. *Journals of Gerontology: Social Sciences* 59B(6): S305–S314.

Calasanti, T.M. (2003). Masculinities and Care Work in Old Age. In S. Arber, K. Davidson, and J. Ginn (Eds.), *Gender and Ageing: Changing Roles and Relationships,* 15–30. Philadelphia: Maidenhead Press.

Calasanti, T., and Bowen, M.E. (2006). Spousal Caregiving and Crossing Gender Boundaries: Maintaining Gendered Identities. *Journal of Aging Studies* 20: 253–63.

Calasanti, T., and King, N. (2005). Firming the Floppy Penis: Age, Class, and Gender Relations in the Lives of Old Men. *Men and Masculinities* 8(1): 3–23.

Campbell, H. (2006). Real Men, Real Locals, and Real Workers: Realizing Masculinity in Small-Town New Zealand. In H. Campbell, M.M. Bell, and M. Finney (Eds.), *Country Boys: Masculinity in Rural Life,* 88–103. University Park: Pennsylvania State University Press.

Campbell, L.D., and Carroll, M.P. (2007). The Incomplete Revolution: Theorizing Gender When Studying Men Who Provide Care to Aging Parents. *Men and Masculnities* 9(4): 491–508.

Campbell, S., and Silverman, P.R. (1996). *Widower: When Men Are Left Alone.* Amityville: Baywood.

Canadian Broadcasting Corporation. (2008). About the Week the Women Went: Can the Men of a Small Alberta Town Survive on Their Own? Retrieved 10 March 2008 from: http://www.cbc.ca/thewomenwent/.

Carr, D. (2004). The Desire to Date and Remarry among Older Widows and Widowers. *Journal of Marriage and the Family* 66: 1051–68.

Charmaz, K. (1994). Identity Dilemmas of Chronically Ill Men. *Sociological Quarterly* 35(2): 269–88.

Charmaz, K. (1991). *Good Days, Bad Days: The Self in Chronic Illness and Time.* New Brunswick: Rutgers University Press.

Coates, J. (2003). *Men Talk: Stories in the Making of Masculinities.* Malden: Blackwell.

Coles, J. (2008). Finding Space in the Field of Masculinities: Lived Experiences of Men's Masculinities. *Journal of Sociology* 44(3): 233–48.

Connell, R.W. (1987). *Gender and Power: Society, the Persons and Sexual Politics.* Cambridge: Polity Press.

Connidis, I.A. (2001). *Family Ties and Aging.* Thousand Oaks: Sage.

Connidis, I.A., and McMullen, J.A. (2002). Sociological Ambivalence and Family Ties: A Critical Perspective. *Journal of Marriage and the Family* 64 (Aug.): 558–67.

Courtney, W.H. (2000a). Behavioral Factors Associated with Disease, Injury and Death among Men: Evidence and Implications for Prevention. *Journal of Men's Studies* 10: 129–42.

Courtney, W.H. (2000b). Constructions of Masculinity and Their Influence on Men's Well-Being: A Theory of Gender and Health. *Social Science and Medicine* 50: 1385–1401.

Crummy, D.B. (2002). *Resilience: The Lived Experience of Elderly Widowers Following the Death of a Spouse.* Ph.D. Dissertation, University of San Diego.

Davidson, K. (2004). Gender Differences in New Partnership Choices and Constraints for Older Widows and Widowers. In K. Davidson and G. Fennell (Eds.), *Intimacy in Later Life,* 65–83. New Brunswick: Transaction.

Davidson, K. (1999). *Gender, Age and Widowhood: How Older Widows and Widowers Differently Realign Their Lives.* Ph.D. Dissertation, Centre for Research on Ageing and Gender, University of Surrey.

Davidson, K., Arber, S., and Ginn, J. (2000). Gendered Meanings of Care Work within Later Life Marital Relationships. *Canadian Journal on Aging* 19(4): 536–53.

Davidson, K., Daly T., and Arber S. (2003a). Exploring the Social Worlds of Older Men. In S. Arber, K. Davidson, and J. Ginn (Eds.), *Gender and Ageing:*

Changing Roles and Relationships, 168–85. Maidenhead: Open University Press.

Davidson, K., Daly T., and Arber S. (2003b). Older Men, Social Integration, and Organisational Activities. *Social Policy and Society* 2(2): 81–9.

de Jong Gierveld, J. (2004). The Dilemma of Repartnering: Considerations of Older Men and Women Entering New Intimate Relationships in Later Life. In K. Davidson and G. Fennell (Eds.), *Intimacy in Later Life,* 85–103. New Brunswick: Transaction.

Doka, K.A., and Martin, T. (2001). Take It Like a Man: Masculine Response to Loss. In Dale A. Lund (Ed.), *Men Coping with Grief,* 37–47. Amityville: Baywood.

Doucet, A. (2008). From Her Side of the Gossamer Wall(s): Reflexivity and Relational Knowing. *Qualitative Sociology* 31(1): 73–87.

Doucet, A. (2007). *Do Men Mother?* Toronto: University of Toronto Press.

Drummond, M., and Smith, J. (2006). Ageing Men's Understanding of Nutrition: Implications for Health. *Journal of Men's Health and Gender* 3(1): 56–60.

Du Plessis, V., Beshiri, R., Bollman, R. D., and Clemenson, H. (1996). 'Definitions of Rural.' Ottawa: Statistics Canada.

Ducat, S.J. (2004). *The Wimp Factor: Gender Gaps, Holy Wars, and the Politics of Anxious Masculinity.* Boston: Beacon Press.

Duneier, M. (1992) *Slim's Table: Race, Respectability, and Masculinity.* Chicago: University of Chicago Press.

Dunlop, B.D., Rothman, M.B., and Rambali, C. (1997). Elderly Men in Retirement Communities. In J.I. Kosberg and L.W. Kaye (Eds.), *Elderly Men: Special Problems and Professional Challenges,* 74–97. New York: Springer.

Edley, N., and Wetherell, M. (1995). *Men in Perspective: Practice, Power and Identity.* London: Prentice-Hall Harvester Wheatsheaf.

Ekerdt, D.J. (1986). The Busy Ethic: Moral Continuity between Work and Retirement. *Gerontologist* 26(3): 239–44.

Feinson, M.C. (1986). Aging Widows and Widowers: Are There Mental Health Differences? *International Journal of Aging and Human Development* 23(4): 241–55.

Field, D., Hockey, J., and Small, N. (1997). *Death, Gender and Ethnicity.* London: Routledge.

Fine, G.A. (1990). Symbolic Interactionism in the Post-Blumerian Age. In G. Ritzer (Ed.), *Frontiers of Social Theory: The New Synthesis,* 117–57. New York: Columbia University Press.

Fingerman, K.L, Hay, E.L., and Birditt, K.S. (2004). The Best of Ties, the Worst of Ties: Problematic and Ambivalent Social Relationships. *Journal of Marriage and the Family* 66 (Aug.): 792–808.

Ford, R.J. (2006). The Casserole Brigade. Available at: www.facebook.com/l/cee7a;robertjohnford.com.

Genoe, R.M. (2004). *Masculinity Theory and Older Men's Leisure Experiences across Their Lifespan*. Ph.D. Dissertation, Dalhousie University, Halifax.

Gershick, T.J., and Miller, A.D. (1995). Coming to Terms: Masculinity and Physical Disability. In M.S. Kimmel and M.A. Messner (Eds.), *Men's Lives*. 3rd ed., 262–75. Boston: Allyn and Bacon.

Gerson, J. M., and Peiss, K. (1985). Boundaries, Negotiation, Consciousness: Reconceptualizing Gender Relations. *Social Problems* 32(4): 317–31.

Gilbar, O., and Dagan, A. (1995). Coping with Loss: Differences between Widows and Widowers of Deceased Cancer Patients. *Omega* 31(3): 207–20.

Glaser, B.G., and Strauss, A. (1965). *Awareness of Dying Contexts*. Chicago: Aldine.

Goffman, E. (1963). *Stigma: Notes on the Management of a Spoiled Identity*. New York: Touchstone Books.

Goffman, E. (1959). *The Presentation of Self in Everyday Life*. New York: Doubleday.

Goldscheider, F.K. (1990). The Aging of the Gender Revolution: What Do We Know and What Do We Need to Know? *Journal of Aging Studies* 12(4): 531–46.

Gorer, G. (1965). *Death, Grief, and Mourning in Contemporary Britain*. London: Cresset Press.

Gross, G., and Blundo, R. (2005). Viagra: Medical Technology Constructing Aging Masculinity. *Journal of Sociology and Social Welfare* 21(1): 85–97.

Gupta, S. (1999). The Effects of Transitions in Marital Status on Men's Performance of Housework. *Journal of Marriage and the Family* 61: 700–11.

Ha, J.-J., Carr, D., Utz, R.L., and Nesse, R. (2006). Older Adults' Perceptions of Intergenerational Support after Widowhood. *Journal of Family Issues* 27(1): 3–30.

Haigh, J. (1999). Put a Cork in the Whine. *Men's Health* 14(8): 100–1.

Harper, D. (2007). Widow. *Online Etymology Dictionary*. Retrieved 6 June 2007 from http://dictionary.reference.com/browse/widow.

Harris, P.B. (2005). The Voices of Husbands and Sons Caring for a Family Member with Dementia. In B.J. Kramer and E.H. Thompson Jr (Eds.), *Men as Caregivers*, 213–33. Amherst: Prometheus Books.

Harris, P.B., and Bichler, J. (1997). *Men Giving Care: Reflections of Husbands and Sons*. New York: Garland.

Henson, K.D., and Rogers, J.K. (2001). 'Why Marcia You've Changed!' Male Clerical Temporary Workers Doing Masculinity in a Feminized Occupation. *Gender and Society* 15(2): 218–38.

Hiekkinen, R.-L. (1996). Experienced Aging as Elucidated by Narratives. In J.E. Birren, G.M. Kenyon, J.-E. Ruth, J.J.R. Schoots, and T. Svensson (Eds.), *Aging and Biography: Explorations in Adult Development*, 187–204. New York: Springer.

Hochschild, A.R. (1989). *The Second Shift: Working Parents and the Revolution at Home*. New York: Viking.

Hoffman, L.W., McManus, K.A., and Brackbill, Y. (1987). The Value of Children to Young and Elderly Parents. *International Journal of Aging and Human Development* 25: 309–22.

Hollander, J.A., and Gordon, H.R. (2006). The Processes of Social Construction in Talk. *Symbolic Interaction* 29(2): 183–212.

Holstein, J.A., and Gubrium, J.F. (1995). *The Active Interview*. Thousand Oaks: Sage.

Hughes, E.C. (1984) [1945]. *The Sociological Eye: Selected Papers*. New Brunswick: Transaction.

Jackson, D., and Mannix, J. (2004). Giving Voice to the Burden of Blame: A Feminist Study of Mothers' Experiences of Mother Blaming. *International Journal of Nursing Practice* 10: 150–8.

Kalish, R.A. (1976). Death and Dying in a Social Context. In R.H. Binstock and E. Shanas (Eds.), *Handbook of Aging and the Social Sciences*, 483–510. New York: Van Nostrand Reinhold.

Kaplan, D. (2006). Public Intimacy: Dynamics of Seduction in Male Homosocial Interactions. *Symbolic Interaction* 28(4): 571–95.

Karlsson, S.G., and Borell, K. (2004). Living Apart Together. In K. Davidson and G. Fennell (Eds.), *Intimacy in Later Life*, 2–18. New Brunswick: Transaction.

Katz, S. (2000). Busy Bodies: Activity, Aging, and the Management of Everyday Life. *Journal of Aging Studies* 14(2): 135–52.

Kaufman, G., and Uhlenberg, P. (1998). Effects of Life Course Transitions on the Quality of Relationships between Adult Children and Their Parents. *Journal of Marriage and the Family* 60(4): 924–39.

Keith, P.M. (1994). A Typology of Orientations toward Household and Marital Roles of Older Men and Women. In Edward H. Thompson (Ed.), *Older Men's Lives*, 141–58. Thousand Oaks: Sage.

Keith, P.M., and Brabaker, T.H. (1979). Male Household Roles in Later Life: A Look at Masculinity and Marital Relationships. *Family Coordinator* 28(4): 497–502.

King, S. (1998). *Bag of Bones*. New York: Scribner.

Kingston, A. (2007). The Sexiest Man Alive. *Maclean's*. 22 Nov. Retrieved 12 March 2008 from www.macleans.ca/culture/lifestyle/article.jsp?content=200711.

Kirsi, T., Hervonen, A., and Jylhä, M. (2000). 'A Man's Gotta Do What a Man's Gotta Do': Husbands as Caregivers to their Demented Wives. A Discourse Analysis. *Journal of Aging Studies* 14(2): 153–69.

Lareau, A. (2000). My Wife Can Tell Me Who I Know: Methodological and Conceptual Problems in Studying Fathers. *Qualitative Sociology* 23(4): 407–33.

Levang, E. (1998). *When Men Grieve: Why Men Grieve Differently and What You Can Do about It*. Minneapolis: Fairview Press.

Loe, M. (2004). Sex and the Senior Woman: Pleasure and Danger in the Viagra Era. *Sexualities* 7(3): 303–26.

Lopata, H.Z. (1996). *Current Widowhood: Myths and Realities*. Thousand Oaks: Sage.

L_uescher, K., and Pillemer, K. (1998). Intergenerational Ambivalence: A New Approach to the Study of Parent-Child Relations in Later Life. *Journal of Marriage and the Family* 60 (May): 413–25.

Lund, D.A., and Caserta, M.S. (2001). When the Unexpected Happens: Husbands Coping with the Deaths of Their Wives. In D.A. Lund (Ed.), *Men Coping with Grief*, 147–67. Amityville: Baywood.

Lund, D.A., Caserta, M.S., and Diamond, M.F. (1993). Spousal Bereavement in Later Life. In M.S. Stroebe, W. Streobe, and R.O. Hansson (Eds.), *Handbook of Bereavement*, 240–54. New York: Cambridge University Press.

Mansfield, H.C. (2007). *Manliness*. New Haven: Yale University Press.

Martin-Matthews, A. (2000). Intergenerational Caregiving: How Apocalyptic and Dominant Demographies Frame the Questions and Shape the Answers. In E.M. Gee and G.M. Gutman (Eds.), *The Overselling of Population Aging: Apocalyptic Demography, Intergenerational Challenges, and Social Policy*, 67–79. Toronto: Oxford University Press.

Martin-Matthews, A. (1991). *Widowhood in Later Life*. Toronto: Butterworths.

Matthews, B., and Beaman, L. (2007). *Exploring Gender in Canada: A Multi-Dimensional Approach*. Toronto: Pearson.

Matthews, S.H. (2000) [1986]. Friendship Styles. In J.F. Gubrium and J.A. Holstein (Eds.), *Aging and Everyday Life*, 155–74. Malden: Blackwell.

Matthews, S.H. (1994). Men's Ties to Siblings in Old Age: Contributing Factors to Availability and Quality. In E.H. Thompson (Ed.), *Older Men's Lives*, 178–96. Thousand Oaks: Sage.

Matthews, S.H. (1986). *Friendships through the Life Course: Oral Biographies in Old Age*. Beverly Hills: Sage

Matthews, S.H. (1979). *The Social World of Old Women: Management of Self-Identity*. Newbury Park: Sage.

McMahon, A. (1999) *Taking Care of Men: Sexual Politics in the Public Mind.* Cambridge: Cambridge University Press.

Meadows, R., and Davidson, K. (2006). Maintaining Masculinities in Later Life: Hegemonic Masculinities and Emphasized Femininities. In T.M. Calasanti and K.F. Slevin (Eds.), *Age Matters: Realigning Feminist Thinking,* 295–312. New York: Routledge.

Moore, A.J., and Stratton, D. (2004). The Current Woman in an Old Widower's Life. In K. Davidson and G. Fennell (Eds.), *Intimacy in Later Life,* 121–42. New Brunswick: Transaction.

Moore, A.J., and Stratton, D.C. (2002). *Resilient Widowers: Older Men Speak for Themselves.* New York: Springer.

Morgan, D.H.J. (1992). *Discovering Men.* London and New York: Routledge.

Moss, S.Z., Moss, M.S., Kilbride, J.E., and Rubinstein, R.L. (2007). Frail Men's Perspectives on Food and Eating. *Journal of Aging Studies* 21(4): 314–24.

Munro, A. (2000) [1989]. Menesteung. In John Updike and Katrina Kennison (Eds.), *The Best American Short Stories of the Century,* 633–51. Boston: Houghton Mifflin.

Nimrod, G., and Adoni, H. (2006). Leisure-Styles and Life Satisfaction among Recent Retirees in Israel. *Ageing and Society* 26: 607–30.

Nydegger, C.N., and Mitteness, L.S. (1991). Fathers and Their Adult Sons and Daughters. In S.K. Pfeifer and M.B. Sussman (Eds.), *Families: Intergenerational and Generational Connections,* 249–66. New York: Haworth Press.

Oldenburg, R. (1989). *The Great Good Place: Cafés, Coffee Shops, Community Centers, Beauty Parlors, General Stores, Bars, Hangouts, and How They Get You through the Day.* New York: Paragon House.

Perren, K., Arber, S., and Davidson, K. (2003). Men's Organizational Affiliations in Later Life: The Influence of Social Class and Marital Status on Informal Group Membership. *Ageing and Society* 23: 69–82.

Peters, C.L., Hooker, K., and Zvonkovic, A.M. (2006). Older Parents' Perceptions of Ambivalence in Relationships with Children. *Family Relations* 55 (Dec.): 539–51.

Powers, E.A., and Bultena, G.L. (1976). Sex Differences in Intimate Friendships of Old Age. *Journal of Marriage and the Family* 38(3): 739–47.

Pratt, T.K. (1982). Island English: The Case of the Disappearing Dialect. In V. Smitheram, D. Milne, and S. Dasgupta (Eds.), *The Garden Transformed: Prince Edward Island 1945–1980,* 231–42. Charlottetown: Ragweed Press.

Rakoff, R.M. (1977). Ideology in Everyday Life: The Meaning of the House. *Politics and Society* 7: 85–104.

Ribeiro, O., Paúl, C., and Nogueira, C. (2007). Real Men, Real Husbands: Caregiving and Masculinities in Later Life. *Journal of Aging Studies* 21(4): 302–13.

Richardson, L. (1985). *The New Other Woman: Contemporary Single Women in Affairs with Married Men.* New York: Free Press.

Ronin, R.A. (2000). *Widowerhood: A Study of Spousal Bereavement and Its Potential for Stimulating Meaning.* Ph.D. Dissertation, California School of Professional Psychology, San Diego.

Rose, H., and Bruce, E. (1995). Mutual Care but Differential Esteem: Caring between Older Couples. In S. Arber and J. Ginn (Eds.), *Connecting Gender and Ageing: A Sociological Approach,* 114–28. Buckingham: Open University Press.

Rosenmayr, L. (1977). The Family: A Source of Hope for the Elderly? In E. Shanas and M.B. Sussman (Eds.), *Family, Bureaucracy, and the Elderly,* 132–57. Durham: Duke University Press.

Rosenthal, C.J. (1985). Kinkeeping in the Familial Division of Labor. *Journal of Marriage and the Family* 47(4): 965–74.

Rubin, R. (2004). Men Talking about Viagra: An Exploratory Study with Focus Groups. *Men and Masculinities* 7(1): 22–30.

Rubinstein, Robert L. (1986). *Singular Paths: Old Men Living Alone.* New York: Columbia University Press.

Russell, C. (2007). What Do Older Women and Men Want? Gender Differences in the 'Lived Experience' of Ageing. *Current Sociology* 55(2): 173–92.

Schwalbe, M.L., and Wolkimir, M. (2001). Interviewing Men. In J.F. Gubrium and J.A. Holstein (Eds.), *Handbook of Interview Research: Context and Method,* 203–19. Thousand Oaks: Sage.

Seale, C. (2002). Cancer Heroics: A Study of News Reports with Particular Reference to Gender. *Sociology* 36(1): 107–26.

Seale, C. (1995). Heroic Death. *Sociology* 29(4): 597–613.

Siebert, D.C., Mutran, E.J., and Reitzes, D.C. (1999). Friendship and Social Support: The Importance of Role Identity to Aging Adults. *Social Work* 6: 522–33.

Silverman, P.R. (1996). Introduction to this New Edition. In S. Campbell and P.R. Silverman, *Widower: When Men Are Left Alone,* 1–16. Amityville: Baywood.

Simmel, G. (1950). *The Sociology of Georg Simmel.* Translated, edited, and with an introduction by Kurt H. Wolff. New York: Free Press.

Slevin, K. F. (2008). Disciplining 'Bodies': The Aging Experience of Older Heterosexual and Gay Men. *Generations* 32(1): 36–42.

Smith, J.A., Braunack-Mayer, A., Wittert, G., and Warin, M. (2007). 'I've Been Independent for So Damn Long': Independence, Masculinity and Aging in a Help-Seeking Context. *Journal of Aging Studies* 21(4): 325–35.

Snow, D.A., and Anderson, L. (1987). Identity Work among the Homeless: The Verbal Construction and Avowal of Personal Identities. *American Journal of Sociology* 92(6): 1336–71.

South, S.J., and Spitze, G. (1994). Housework in Marital and Nonmarital Households. *American Sociological Review* 59: 327–47.

Spector-Mersel, G. (2006). Never-Ending Stories: Western Hegemonic Masculinity Scripts. *Journal of Gender Studies* 15(1): 67–82.

Statistics Canada. (2007). Internet Site, CANSIM Table 053-0001. Retrieved 6 May 2009 from http://www40.statcan.gc.ca/l01/cst01/famil04eng.htm.

Statistics Canada. (2004). Internet Site, CANSIM, Table 051-0010. Retrieved 12 July 2004 from www.statcan.ca/english/Pgdb/famil01a.htm.

Statistics Canada. (2003). *Canadian Social Trends.* 'Update on Families.' Summer. Retrieved 5 May 2009 from http://www.statcan.ca/english/freepub/11-008-XIE/2003001/articles/629.pdf.

Steeves, R.H., and Kahn, D.L. (2005). Experiences of Bereavement in Rural Elders. *Journal of Hospice and Palliative Nursing* 7(4): 197–205.

Stevens, N. (2004). Re-engaging: New Partnerships in Late-Life Widowhood. In K. Davidson and G. Fennell (Eds.), *Intimacy in Later Life*, 47–64. New Brunswick: Transaction.

Stevens, N. (1995). Gender and Adaptation to Widowhood in Later Life. *Ageing and Society* 15(1): 37–58.

Strain, L. (2001). Senior Centres: Who Participates. *Canadian Journal on Aging* 20(4): 471–91.

Stratton, D.C., and Moore, A.J. (2003). Resilience in Jewish Widowers. *Social Work Forum* 36: 5–23.

Thomas, J.L. (1994). Older Men as Fathers and Grandfathers. In E.H. Thompson Jr (Ed.), *Older Men's Lives*, 197–217. Thousand Oaks: Sage.

Thompson, E.H. Jr. (2006). Images of Old Men's Masculinity: Still a Man? *Sex Roles* 55: 633–48.

Thompson, N. (1997). Masculinity and Loss. In D. Field, J. Hockey, and N. Small (Eds.), *Death, Gender and Ethnicity*, 76–88. London: Routledge.

Tignoli, J. (1980). Male Friendship and Intimacy across the Lifespan. *Family Relations* 29: 273–9.

Tropper, J. (2007). *How to Talk to a Widower.* New York: Delacourt Press.

Trovato, F., and Halli, S.S. (1983). Regional Differences in Family Size: The Case of the Atlantic Provinces in Canada. *Rural Sociology* 48(2): 271–90.

van den Hoonaard, D. K. (2009a). Widowers' Strategies of Self-Representation in an Interview Situation: A Sociological Analysis. *Ageing and Society* 29(2): 257–76.

van den Hoonaard, D. K. (2009b). I Was the Man: The Challenges of Masculinity for Older Men. In *Masculinity: Gender Roles, Characteristics and Coping*, 69–84. Hauppauge: Nova Science Publishers.

van den Hoonaard, D.K. (2007). Aging and Masculinity: A Topic Whose Time Has Come. *Journal of Aging Studies* 21: 277–80.

van den Hoonaard, D.K. (2006). I Was the Man: Older Widowers' Strategies of Self-Representation. Paper presented at Studying Everyday Life: Symbolic Interaction and Ethnographic Research Conference, Niagara Falls, Ontario, 16–18 May.

van den Hoonaard, D. K. (2003). Expectations and Experiences of Widowhood. In J.F. Gubrium and J.A. Holstein (Eds.), *Ways of Aging*, 182–99. Malden: Blackwell.

van den Hoonaard, D.K. (2001). *The Widowed Self: The Older Woman's Journey through Widowhood*. Waterloo: Wilfrid Laurier University Press.

van den Hoonaard, D.K. (1997). Identity Foreclosure: Women's Experiences of Widowhood as Expressed in Autobiographical Accounts. *Ageing and Society* 17: 533–51.

van den Hoonaard, D.K. (1994). Paradise Lost: Widowhood in a Florida Retirement Community. *Journal of Aging Studies* 8(2): 121–32.

van den Hoonaard, D.K. (1992). *The Aging of a [Florida] Retirement Community*. Ph.D. dissertation, Loyola University of Chicago.

van den Hoonaard, W.C. (1997). *Working with Sensitizing Concepts*. Thousand Oaks: Sage.

Weber, M. (1949). *The Methodology of the Social Sciences*. Trans. by E.A. Shils and H.A. Finch. Glencoe: Free Press.

West, C., and Zimmerman, D.H. (1987). Doing Gender. *Gender and Society* 1(2): 125–15.

Wilson, G. (2000). *Understanding Old Age: Critical and Global Perspectives*. London: Sage.

Wister, A.V., and Strain, L. (1986). Social Support and Well-Being: A Comparison of Older Widows and Widowers. *Canadian Journal on Aging* 5(3): 205–20.

Wright, P.H. (1988). Gender Differences in Adults' Same- and Cross-Gender Friendships. In R.G. Adams and R. Bleiszner (Eds.), *Older Adult Friendship: Structure and Process*, 197–221. Newbury Park: Sage.

Wright, P.H. (1982). Men's Friendships, Women's Friendships and the Alleged Inferiority of the Latter. *Sex Roles* 8(1): 1–20.

Index